941·02

CW00435393

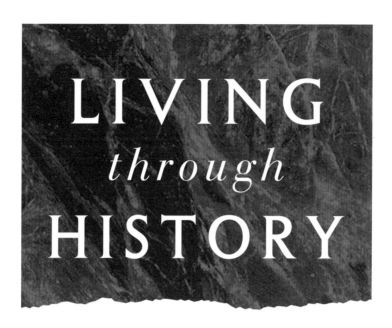

LIVING *through* HISTORY

Medieval Realms

Nigel Kelly, Rosemary Rees
and Jane Shuter

Heinemann

CONTENTS

| 1066 | 1100 | 1150 | 1200 | 1250 | 1300 | 1350 | 1400 | 1450 | 1500 |

The medieval period

The twentieth century

| 1900 | 1950 | 2000 |

This book covers many hundreds of years, from 1066 to 1485 (compare it with the twentieth century on the time-line above). This period is sometimes known as the Middle Ages, or the medieval period. However, it would be wrong to imagine that the Middle Ages either began or ended on any particular date. The Middle Ages is in fact just a kind of nick-name given to the period between the end of the Roman Empire and the Renaissance.

There are ways in which people in medieval England were very different from people in England now. One difference is that everybody in the country believed in the Christian God, and the power of his saints. Most people worshipped him in the same way. Now people follow lots of different religions and they worship in different ways. Some have no religion at all. But there are ways in which people were the same as they are now. Most people worked for a living, while a few rich people did not have to. They all needed food, drink and shelter.

Source A

An illustration from a book made in about 1410. Some people are out hawking (hunting smaller birds with hawks for fun). Others are working in the fields.

Source B

An example of the dangers of not believing in a saint, from a book written in about 1200:

An abbot of Bury St. Edmunds [where St. Edmund was buried] wanted to be sure that the head of St. Edmund, which had been chopped off, had really been miraculously re-united with his body as had been said.

So he had the tomb opened. He told one man to hold the head of the saint and another man to hold the saint's feet. The men tugged, but the body really was together.

The abbot was punished for his disbelief. He was struck down with terrible shaking in both hands, so great that he could not eat nor drink, and soon after he died.

St. Edmund

St. Edmund (who died in about 870) was king of the Saxon Kingdom of East Anglia from about 855 until his death.

King Edmund was killed by Viking invaders, probably while he was their prisoner, although some people claim he died fighting.

After he died, people spoke of miraculous cures at the place where he was buried. He was made a saint.

Source C

A Frenchman, writing about England during the medieval period:

In England, as well as in several other countries, the lords have great power over the common people, who are their workers.

The common people have to plough the fields of their masters, to sow and harvest the crops and carry them to the barns. They must cut hay and collect wood and do all sorts of jobs. In some parts of the country the lords work the people much harder, especially in Kent, Essex and Bedfordshire.

Salisbury Cathedral in modern times. Cathedrals took hundreds of workers many years to finish, and they cost a lot of money to build. Most cathedrals in Europe date from medieval times, and most are still standing, unlike medieval homes.

Source D

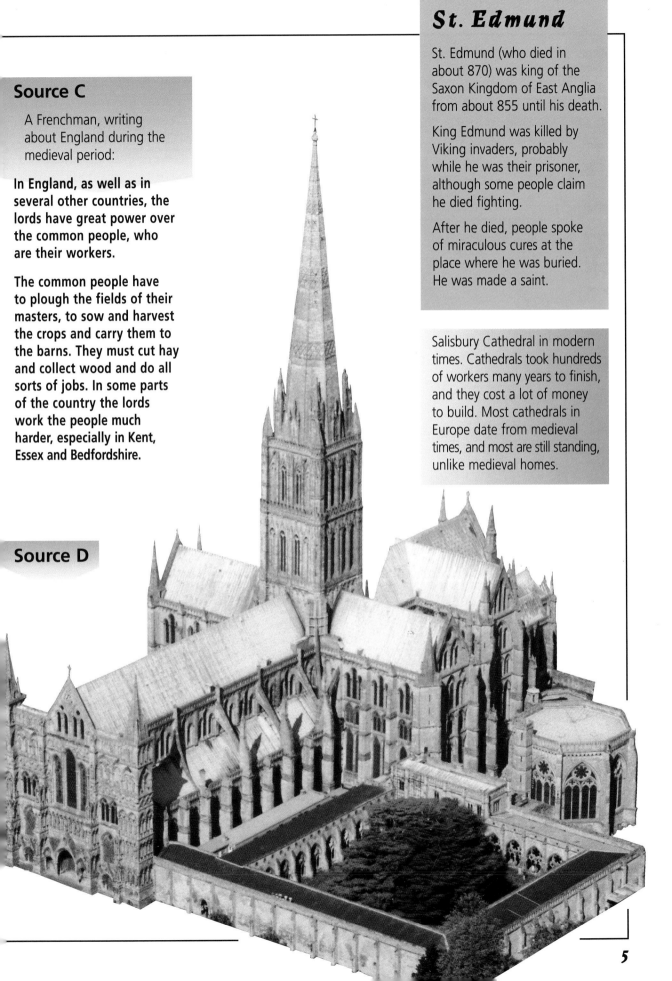

Ideas and events

This book looks at some of the most important ideas and events of the medieval period. There are some ideas that run like a thread all through the book, and some questions that you constantly need to ask yourself as you go through.

Who is in control?

One of the most important questions is 'Who is in control?' There were tussles for control all through the medieval period, involving kings, lords and churchmen. Sometimes kings tried to rule alone. The lords would then try to force them to accept advice.

Strong kings, weak kings

The character of a king affected the way the country was run. A strong king held the country together. The lords were happy to work with him, so were churchmen. But a king could be too strong, and could push the lords or the Church into acting against him by being unreasonable.

Kings could also be too weak, then there was a scramble for power between the most important lords, and sometimes **civil war.**

Source E

The King and the Church

Kings ruled their own countries, but they did not run the Church. The Church in England was part of the Roman Catholic Church. The head of the Church was the Pope, who lived in Rome. The Pope was in charge of all churchmen, and through them all Christians in all the Christian countries in Europe. As long as the Pope and the English kings wanted the same things, the Pope's power was not a problem. When they disagreed there was trouble. All European kings were in the same boat.

The most important churchmen crown a new king. But does he trust them? Will he try to control the Church, or will they be able to tell him what to do?

Part of Europe?

England had always been caught up in events in the rest of the world, especially in Europe. The Romans and the Danes had invaded England as part of a wider sweep across Europe. The Christian Church drew England into Europe with other Christian nations.

All through the medieval period the kings of England held different areas of land in Europe, mostly in modern France. But by 1500 all that was left was Calais. The English kings tried to get these lands back, but with the end of the medieval period came a change in the way English kings saw England. They no longer saw England as part of a wider, Europe-based empire. They were kings of England, trying to get extra land for an English empire.

Ordinary people

As well as looking at who was in control, we focus on ordinary people in England at the time. What did people believe? How did this affect their lives? It would make a big difference to how you behaved if you believed, as people did in medieval times, that God was watching every move you made, and that unless you repented you would be punished for bad behaviour by burning in Hell forever.

You will also look at the day-to-day lives of ordinary people. What was it like to live in a village? What was it like to live in a town? You will look at how people lived, what sort of work they did, what they ate and drank and what they bought at the market.

Things to think about

As you go through this book, there are two questions you need to keep asking yourself:

- who is in control?
- how does this affect ordinary people?

A medieval view of Hell. All Christians believed that this was a real destination for sinners who were not sorry for their sins.

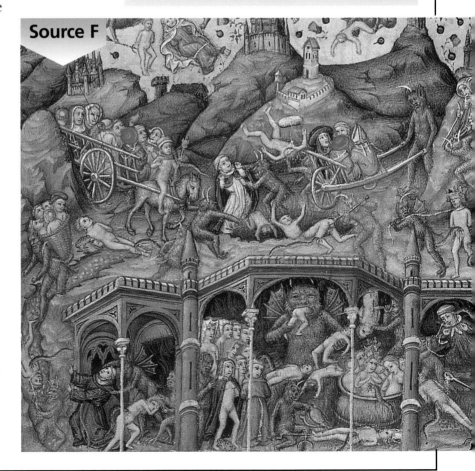

Source F

In 1066 King Edward the Confessor died. He had no son to take over as king. As he lay dying, he said that Harold Godwinson, an English earl, should be king after him (at least, that's what Harold said; we don't really know). Despite this, two other people claimed the throne of England. They both invaded in 1066. Why?

At this time in England, kings were elected by the most powerful English earls. If a strong king had a suitable son, then the son was likely to get elected. If not, the earls chose the strongest person with a claim to the throne. Edward may have named Harold Godwinson, but the earls did not have to accept him. There were several people who claimed the right to be the next king after Edward. The boxes below outline the main claimants' reasons for saying they should be king.

HARALD HARDRADA, KING OF NORWAY

Claimed to have a right to the throne dating from when England had a Danish king

A good warrior

EARL HAROLD GODWINSON

A powerful land-holder and Earl of Wessex

Edward's brother-in-law

Claimed Edward offered him the throne in 1066

A good warrior

NORWAY

N
S

ENGLAND

0   200 miles
0   300 km

NORMANDY

WILLIAM, DUKE OF NORMANDY

Claimed Edward promised him the crown in 1051

Claimed Harold Godwinson had sworn an oath to help William become king

Supported by the Pope

A good warrior

Who did Edward choose to be king?

Edward may have promised the throne to at least two of the claimants. Despite this, the earls made Harold Godwinson king the day after Edward died. This was very quick. Perhaps Edward chose Harold as he lay dying. Perhaps the earls, hearing that Harald Hardrada was about to invade, chose Harold Godwinson, hoping he could unite people to drive Harald Hardrada away. This certainly happened.

Harold's first threat

Harold was crowned king in January 1066. In September, Hardrada invaded Northumbria and was accepted as king there. Harold marched north with an army. There was a fierce battle at Stamford Bridge, and Harald Hardrada was killed. One threat to King Harold was removed. But he still had to face William of Normandy.

Scenes from the Bayeux Tapestry, begun after 1066 and finished in 1077. It was ordered to be made by Bishop Odo of Bayeux, William's half-brother. The first scene shows Harold promising to support William. The second shows Edward dying.

Source B

One modern historian's view of Edward the Confessor.

Edward had some ability, but did not have the energy and ruthless determination of a successful king. He was not a great warrior, and never managed to control the earls. Duke William seemed to be Edward's choice for his successor. At the end of 1065 Edward was known to be dying and the vultures began to collect. What happened that Christmas we will never know.

Broken promises

We know that, in 1064, Edward the Confessor sent some of his lords (including Harold Godwinson) to William's court in Normandy. They spoke in private. On Edward the Confessor's death they both claimed the throne, and both accused the other of breaking a solemn oath (promise). Harold said William agreed to support him as king of England when Edward the Confessor died. William said that Harold promised to support him as the next king. We have no way of knowing who was telling the truth.

Source A

A modern picture of the Battle of Hastings drawn by Jason Askew.

The Battle of Hastings 14 October 1066

In April 1066, William of Normandy started putting together an army to invade England. William was determined to be King of England. Harold knew this. The most likely time for a Norman invasion was autumn, when the harvest had been gathered in and before the winter storms began. By September Harold was ready for whatever William could throw at him.

A serious distraction

But Harold had not expected Harald Hardrada to invade from Norway in September 1066. Harold had to march north to defeat Harald. At the Battle of Stamford Bridge Harold's Saxon army fought magnificently. They killed Hardrada, 5,000 Danes and sank 276 of his 300 ships. Only 500 Danes escaped.

Invasion!

The day after the battle the Normans invaded. Harold Godwinson marched south with his Saxon army. They were well-trained and experienced fighters. All was far from lost. Harold and his army arrived in London at the end of 6 October. It had taken them just 6 days to march 200 miles. On 11 October Harold left London after resting his troops and gathering more forces.

Preparing for battle

Harold and his army took up position on Senlac Hill, on the other side of a valley north-west of Hastings. Senlac was a steep slope with woods behind it. William seems to have been able to force Harold into fighting in a very tight spot. This gave Harold and his men little chance, if they should need it, of a safe retreat.

HARO L D·REX· INTERFEC TVS·EST

The Bayeux Tapestry is the earliest source of information we have about the Battle of Hastings. This scene from the Tapestry shows Harold being killed. This is what *Harold rex interfectus est* means. But which is Harold?

At nine o'clock on the morning of the 14th, the Normans began to advance. Spears and arrows flew in all directions. The Normans hacked away at the Saxons with swords and lances; the tremendous power of Saxon axeblows cut through Norman **chain-mail**. Both sides fought on foot, although the Normans also used horses later in the day with tremendous effect. The Normans wanted to batter holes in the Saxon **shield wall**; the Saxons wanted to chop the Normans to pieces. Suddenly there was a rumour that William was dead. He wasn't – and he took off his helmet and stood up in his stirrups to shout to his men. Then William and his half-brother, Bishop Odo, started a furious cavalry charge. Normans soldiers on horseback charged at the Saxons just when the Saxons thought they were winning.

Time and time again the Normans used this technique to break through the Saxon shield wall. Gradually the Saxon line broke up and the Saxons were pushed back. At dusk the Saxon army fell back into the shelter of the trees. Harold's bodyguards were left to fight on alone. They formed a semi-circle around Harold. The situation was desperate. According to one tradition recorded in the Bayeux Tapestry, Harold was struck in the eye with an arrow and then stabbed by a Norman knight. Some said that his body was hacked about so badly that it could only be identified by his mistress, Edith Swan-neck.

But had William won the crown of England? Was one battle enough?

Struggles for power

The English and Normans were struggling for power well before 1066!

Harold Godwinson and his father had helped Edward the Confessor become king. This gave them a hold over him. They made him marry Harold's sister. The Normans had a hold over Edward too. They had kept him safe while the Vikings ruled England. He had lived in Normandy since he was eight, so he was, in some ways, more Norman than English.

Sometimes Edward favoured one side, sometimes the other. No one quite managed to completely control him.

In 1085 a German monk wrote that William had *sent almost all the English bishops into exile, and the lords to their death. He forced the wives and daughters of the English lords to marry the newcomers* [Normans]. Did William really treat everyone so badly?

William becomes king

William had hoped to be accepted as king at once. But the earls held out against him. So William marched to London. He ruthlessly put down any opposition on his way, burning whole villages and towns. The earls were forced to accept him as king. He was crowned on Christmas Day, almost exactly a year after Edward died. But, as Harold Godwinson's experience showed, being crowned king did not make you safe. Even being accepted as king in the south was just the first step. William was not King of England yet, and he knew it. He had to get control of the whole country, and keep it. There were three steps in this process:

1 Take over the land, using as much force as was needed.
2 Use force to make sure that people stayed loyal.
3 Change the way the country is run to make sure that people stayed loyal.

Building castles

Castles were vital to William's takeover. Wherever his army took control they built castles to:

- remind people of the power of the Normans
- keep Normans safe in hostile areas
- have a base from which to launch new attacks.

Source A

Orderic Vitalis, a Norman monk, wrote this about the actions of William's army in the north of England.

William collected crops, animals, food and belongings and burned them all. Every living thing north of the River Humber was destroyed. Over 100,000 people, men and women, young and old, died of hunger. I have often praised William, but I cannot excuse his leaving both the innocent and the guilty to slowly starve to death.

Source B

The Bayeux Tapestry showing William's soldiers taking villagers' animals and setting light to another village. It was usual to behave like this to enemies. What horrified people about William's behaviour in the north of England was the scale of it, and the fact that he treated everyone badly, not just those who resisted him.

William eventually beat down most resistance, though it took longest in the north and the eastern fens (marshland). He built castles to keep control. If he needed to pull down villages and towns for this, he did so. He brought in Normans to take over positions of power. He killed any English earls who stood against him – over half of the English earls in 1066 were executed. Women from the families of these earls were forced either to marry Normans or become nuns. In 1085, a survey of the whole country showed there were just two English earls who still held their old places of power. The rest of the country was held by Normans.

The spread of Norman control by 1070.

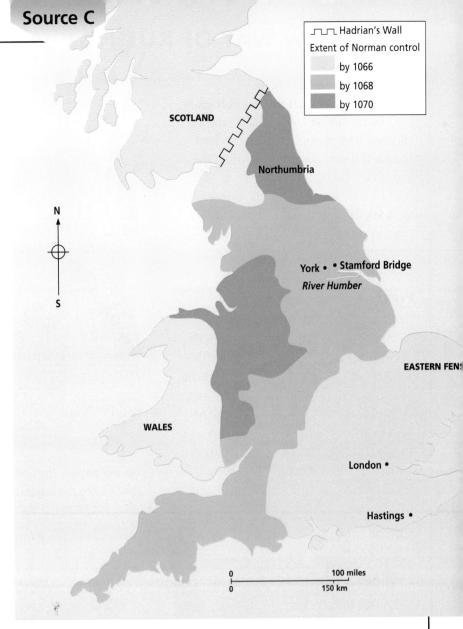

Hadrian's Wall

Extent of Norman control
by 1066
by 1068
by 1070

SCOTLAND

Northumbria

York • • Stamford Bridge
River Humber

EASTERN FENS

WALES

London •

Hastings •

0   100 miles
0   150 km

DOMVS: IN
CENDITVR:

Orderic Vitalis

Orderic Vitalis was born in Atcham, near Shrewsbury, in 1075. He spent almost all of his life in the Norman Abbey of St. Evroul. He was sent to St. Evroul at the age of ten. Even at the age of fifty he could remember the awful moment of his departure: *my father, weeping, gave me, a weeping child, into the care of the monk Reginald, and sent me away into exile for the love of God, and never saw me again*. Orderic is famous for the book he began in 1114 and finished in 1141. It is called *The Ecclesiastic History of England and Normandy*. He died in 1143.

William's new system

Despite the fact that the English earls had sworn to be loyal to William, he did not trust them. After all, he had invaded their country and killed the king they had chosen to rule it. He had to take away the earls' power, so he took away their land. William set up a system of government where he had complete control. William said that the king owned everything.

Foreign ways

William brought in a group of Normans whom he trusted to run the country. He rewarded them with the land that he had taken away from the English earls. This new ruling group were foreigners, with different ways and a different language. William made sure they were loyal to him, by taking away their lands if they were not.

William's changes were made to make sure he kept control.

Source A

An illustration, from about 1400. William is giving land taken from the English Earl of Mercia to his son-in-law, Alan of Brittany. Alan first has to kneel and swear an oath of **fealty** (a faithful promise to be loyal to the King).

What was England worth?

In 1085 William decided to find out what England was worth. This was called the Domesday Survey. He sent people all over the country to ask:

- the name of each place
- who held it in 1066 and in 1085
- what it was worth in 1066 and in 1085
- how much farmland, woodland and land for grazing it had
- how many people lived there
- how many ploughs there were
- how many mills there were.

How the **feudal system** worked. ▶

The King

gives lots of land to

give loyalty and soldiers to

Norman Lords and Churchmen

give soldiers o money to hire soldiers to

give some land to

Norman and English knights and earls

give a house and a garden to

work for or give rent to

Peasants an Tenants

WALTHEOF: AN ENGLISH EARL

Waltheof was a English earl. He was half Danish. He may have fought at Hastings and was taken to Normandy as a hostage by William in 1067. By 1069 he was free and joined a Danish attack on York. William of Malmesbury, the historian, wrote in 1130:

Waltheof killed many Normans in the battle for York, cutting off their heads as they entered the gate. But after York fell he gave himself up and swore fealty. He married Judith, the King's niece, and was honoured with the King's friendship.

Changing his mind?

But despite this Waltheof joined a plot against William, which was found out. Waltheof was put in prison, where he spent hours praying. He swore he was innocent and begged William to let him leave prison and become a monk.

Then, in 1075, the Danes threatened to invade. Many people (including Waltheof's wife, Judith) told William that Waltheof had told the Danes to come. He was eventually beheaded in 1076. Many people thought he had been set up.

There were stories that his head and body had miraculously rejoined after death. This was a common story told about people who were thought to have been unfairly executed (see Source B on page 4). The abbey where he was buried became a place of pilgrimage (a place that people visited because they thought it was holy). William of Malmesbury added:

Perhaps the King may be excused for being severe against the English, for he found hardly any of them to be faithful.

The Domesday Survey

William's survey of England (see **What was England worth?**) was useful in many ways. It told him how rich the country was. This allowed him to work out how much tax each place had to pay. He could also work out how many knights each place should send him if he needed to call an army together.

Effects on the English

So how did the Norman invasion affect ordinary English people? This depended on where they lived and who took control there. People from towns or villages burnt by the Normans (or pulled down to build castles) probably felt the invasion was devastating. But people in out-of-the-way places may have hardly noticed the arrival of the Normans. Some people may even have had a change for the better, if the new Norman lord was fairer than the old English one.

What about the Normans?

The Normans settled down in different ways, depending on their nature and how the local people reacted to them. Some Normans married English wives, learned the language and fitted in. Others did not try. They saw Normandy as home. England was a foreign country. The English were enemies who had to be forced to obey.

William of Malmesbury

William of Malmesbury was born in about 1095. He spent his whole life, from the age of ten, in the abbey of Malmesbury. He wrote several histories of England, a biography of St. Dunstan and a history of Glastonbury. He tried to be balanced in his history writing. There are places in his books where it is clear that he is on one side rather than the other. But, unlike other writers at the time who pretended to be unbiased, William usually admits it!

While the king was away, Bishop Odo [William's half-brother] *built castles throughout the land, oppressing* [being cruel to] *the unhappy people, and things went ever from bad to worse.* This was written in the **Anglo-Saxon Chronicle**. What did these castles look like?

The picture below was drawn by John James in 1994. Does it give us a proper picture of an early Norman castle? How did he know what to draw? How could he have found out about these castles? Some of the things he might have used to help him are:

- modern history books written about the time
- modern books that show clothes that people wore in the past
- the Bayeux Tapestry and pictures from the time
- descriptions of castles from the time
- **excavations** (dug-up remains) of early castles.

Source B

A monk called Lawrence of Durham wrote this description of Durham Castle some time between 1090 and 1149. It is one of the few written descriptions of an early Norman castle in Britain.

On a mound of rising earth there is a flat top and a castle that keeps watch over all the land around it. From its first gate the wall rises higher than the outer ditch. The keep, on a solid earth mound, has even higher walls. Inside the keep is a strong tower, higher even than the keep. It has four posts at each corner, with a walkway around the wall. You reach the keep by a bridge, by steps which lead to a platform that runs around the tower.

Source A

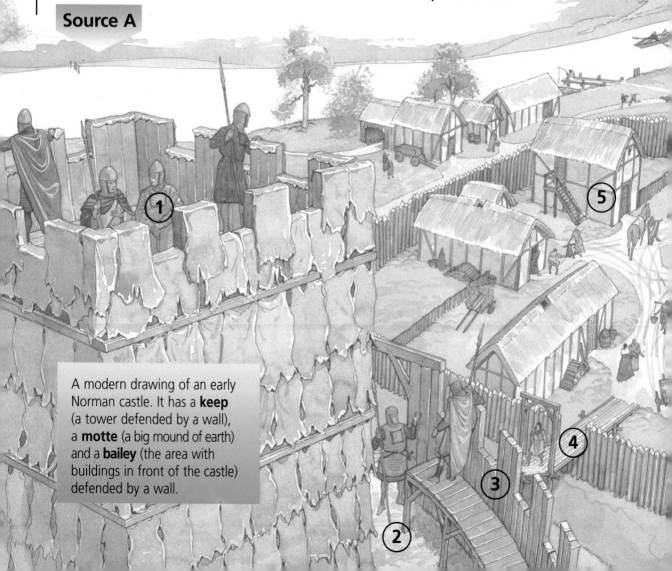

A modern drawing of an early Norman castle. It has a **keep** (a tower defended by a wall), a **motte** (a big mound of earth) and a **bailey** (the area with buildings in front of the castle) defended by a wall.

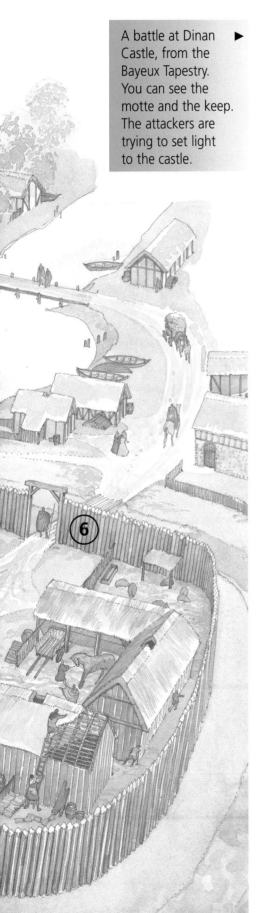

A battle at Dinan Castle, from the Bayeux Tapestry. You can see the motte and the keep. The attackers are trying to set light to the castle.

▶

Source C

Source D

Some of the findings of Robert Higham and Philip Barker, two modern historians who have studied timber castles.

Castles built of wood, sticks and straw leave few traces to study. There are 'ghost' remains of postholes [where the rotting wood has changed the natural colour of the soil] but not much evidence of anything above the ground. From looking at some pieces of mud, we think some wooden castles had a mud layer on the outside.

A temporary solution?

Historians used to think that timber castles were just a temporary solution to the problem of defence. They were quick to put up. This was a good thing. But, the historians said, wood rots, or is a fire hazard. As soon as things settled down the Normans either built stone replacements for timber castles or just abandoned them altogether.

New evidence suggests that this did not always happen. The Normans did build stone castles. Some timber castles were abandoned. But there were several, like Hen Domen on the Welsh borders, that were used well into the thirteenth century. Archaeologists have pointed out that some of these castle walls were plastered. When wood has a covering of plaster, it is less likely to rot or burn.

Today there are lots of different sorts of Christians: Anglicans and Quakers, Methodists, Catholics and many others. In medieval times all Christians in Europe belonged to one church – the Catholic Church – led by the Pope in Rome. The church was very powerful. It was a great landowner; it was extremely rich and influenced many kings and emperors. But the real strength of the church was the power it had over the minds of ordinary people.

The walls of most churches were covered with brightly coloured paintings like this. They reminded ordinary people, who mostly couldn't read or write, about the horrors of hell and the joys of heaven. This wall painting is in the church at Wenhaston, Suffolk. It is called the Doom Painting. Can you find St. Michael? He is weighing people's souls to see if they are good enough to go to heaven. If they aren't, a devil is waiting to take them to hell.

God, heaven and hell

Death was very close to medieval people. Adults died at a much younger age than they do now. A person was very old at forty. Most parents watched some of their children die. Famines, wars, diseases and plagues killed thousands. People must have wondered about the meaning of life. The teaching of the Christian Church gave people the answer. Death was not the end. It was the beginning of everlasting life in heaven with God. People could get to heaven if they followed the teachings of Christ, and were free from sin. Those who were sinful and had not asked for forgiveness went to hell. There they were tormented by devils for ever. It was the church, of course, which explained how Christ wanted people to behave, and decided whether or not their sins were forgiven.

Source A

What was Christendom?

Christendom was that part of the world where most people were Christians. In medieval times, nearly everyone living in Europe was a Christian and belonged to the Catholic Church. There were Christians in other parts of the world, but most of Christendom was in Europe.

In other parts of the world there were people who believed just as deeply in their own religion as Christians did in theirs. There were also Jews in nearly every European country and they followed the ancient faith of Judaism. Christians believed their religion was the one true religion. They called people who followed other religions **infidels**. Christians looked at the world entirely from their own point of view. Jerusalem, their Holy City, was at the centre of the world, and they drew maps to prove it!

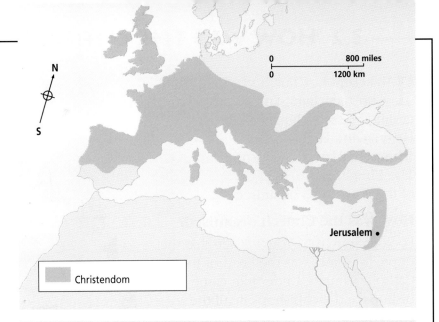

Jerusalem •

Christendom

Christendom in about 1200.

The medieval world

Medieval people did not have the technology to explore or map the world that we have. Parts were undiscovered (such as Australia). Other parts could only be guessed at. Medieval maps show the places they knew about, drawn as accurately as they could measure.

Source B

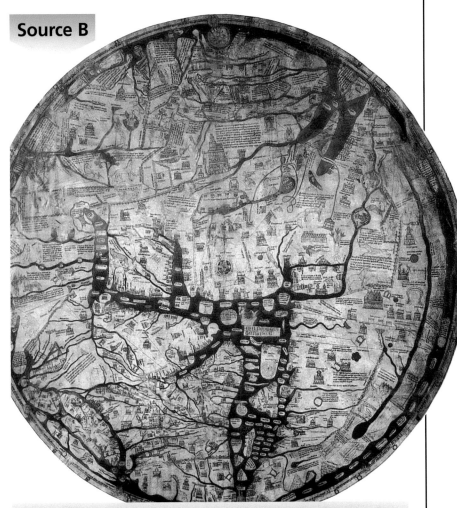

This Mappa Mundi (map of the world) is now in Hereford Cathedral. It was drawn in the 1200s and shows Jerusalem at the centre of the world.

The Catholic Church made sure that all Christians living in Christendom were taught the same things about God, about Heaven and Hell and about Jesus Christ whom they believed was the son of God. The Church was able to do this because of the way it was organised.

How was the Church organised?

Look at Source A. You will see that the Pope, in Rome, was the head of the Catholic Church. Under him came the bishops and archbishops in all the countries of Christendom, including England. Under the bishops and archbishops came the parish (local) priests. There were thousands of parish priests throughout Christendom. They had day-to-day contact with the men, women and children who lived on manors, in villages and in towns. Through its teachings and organisation the Catholic Church was able to influence people's beliefs. This made it very powerful.

Church land

The Church was powerful in other ways, too. It owned a lot of land throughout Christendom. This made the Church very wealthy. Added to this, when rich people died, they often left money, gold and silver and precious jewels to the Church. In this way they hoped to speed up their time in purgatory and get to heaven more quickly.

Running the country

Many bishops and archbishops held important positions in the government of their own countries. This could lead to enormous problems. Some churchmen had to choose between their loyalty to the Pope and their loyalty to their ruler when Church and State disagreed. All Christians were supposed to obey the Pope. What if everyone sided with the Pope against the King?

Source A

Abbots and Archbishops

Priors and Bishops

Friars and Parish Priests

Monks and Nuns

Ordinary people

This shows how the medieval Catholic Church was organised.

Purgatory

This was a place where people who were going to get into Heaven had to wait while all the bad things they had done in their lives were gradually wiped out. People who were still alive could help their friends and relatives speed up their time in purgatory. There were many ways in which they could do this, and the Catholic Church said what they were. They could, for example, go on pilgrimages (visits to holy places), say special prayers and light special candles.

Priests

Most villages had a parish church and a parish priest. The priest, as you have seen, had to make sure everyone knew and followed the teaching of the Catholic Church. It was especially important that he was able to explain things clearly because all church services were held in Latin, a language few people understood.

But priests had other work to do. They visited sick people. They gave food and clothes to the poor. They had to keep the parish records up to date. Priests, unlike most people, could read and write. They recorded the names of everyone who was baptised and married in their church and buried in their churchyard. They also had to write down when these things happened. Some priests waited until the end of the year, and then tried to remember who had married whom, which babies had been born and who had died. They often got things a bit wrong!

Working on the land

Most priests worked hard. As well as running his parish, the priest worked the **glebe** land – land which belonged to the Church. Priests grew the same crops and bred the same animals as everyone else. They argued about prices at market like everyone else. Priests had to make sure everyone paid their **tithe**. This was a tax which said that people had to hand over one tenth of everything they produced to the Church. There were all sorts of local taxes too, which people had to pay their Church either in goods, or money or work. When a person died, the Church could claim his second best animal. All this had to be worked out and recorded by the parish priest.

Church and country

William de Kestevene worked for the King, as well as the Church. This often happened. Churchmen were among the very few people taught to read and write at the time. It was usual to give them government jobs, which needed these skills.

The more important a man's job in the government became, the more important his job in the Church became, too. Important people could have several Church and government jobs.

WILLIAM DE KESTEVENE

William de Kestevene was the parish priest of North Mymms, in Hertfordshire between June 1344 and October 1369, when he died. This brass shows him in the clothes he wore when he took Mass.

William was not a typical priest. He came from a rich family and, before he became a priest, he worked for the King.

In 1337 William bought a quarter of the manor of North Mymms, and in 1344 he became the village parish priest.

Very few priests could afford to have a brass made of themselves. But in his will William left money for a brass to be put over his burial place inside his church. Below is the brass.

Pilgrims

All sorts of people went on pilgrimages. They travelled to places they believed were holy. They went because they wanted to show other people how close they were to God; to ask for a special favour or to be cured of a dreadful disease. Some people went simply to give thanks for something good that had happened to them.

The most holy place in the world for Christians was Jerusalem. Next came Rome, home of the Pope. But ordinary people did not have the time or money to travel abroad. They went to holy places in England instead. These holy places were usually **shrines** in a church or cathedral where there was relic of a saint. This might be a lock of hair, a piece of bone or a tooth.

Holy Days

The Church said that there were certain days in each year which were specially holy. Some of these holy days were days dedicated to certain saints and were kept in some parts of England and not others. Some days were for celebrating festivals like Christmas, Easter and **Whitsun** which everyone kept. The church said that on these days people should go to **Mass** in their local church and should not go to work. Afterwards, people were supposed to go to religious events, like plays, based on Bible stories. Some **craft guilds** put on **miracle plays** in the streets. They tried to out-do each other by the magnificence of their costumes and the scenes they acted on beautifully decorated wagons.

Source A

In about 1386 an English poet called Geoffrey Chaucer wrote a long poem about different people making a pilgrimage to Canterbury. It is called *The Canterbury Tales*. This is part of what he wrote about the beginning of the pilgrimage. The 'martyr' is Thomas Becket.

When in April the sweet showers fall
Then people long to go on pilgrimages
And specially, from every county's end
In England, down to Canterbury they wend [go]
To seek the holy blissful martyr, quick
To give his help to them when they were sick.

At night there came into that hostelry
Some nine and twenty in a company
Of various folk, and they were pilgrims all
That towards Canterbury meant to ride.

Source B

This badge was worn by all pilgrims who visited Canterbury. The little pouch is supposed to contain some of St. Thomas Becket's blood (see pages 34–5).

Desperate for a relic!

Some bishops wanted to have shrines in their cathedrals in order to make them more important. In the 1100s Bishop Hugh of Lincoln visited a French monastery.

While he was there he managed to get hold of two bones from the body of St. Mary Magdalene – by gnawing away at her arm until the bones fell off!

Local fun

However, not everyone behaved in holy ways on holy days! People often went to their local churchyard for singing, dancing and drinking. The church, after all, was a meeting place. The church and churchyard were used for many more things than they are now.

If everyone kept all the Church's holy days, people would have over fifty days' holiday each year! This just didn't happen. **Reeves** had to keep the manor accounts, and these show how many holidays lords allowed their peasants. Most peasants usually had Sundays as a holy day and around fifteen other holy days. Everyone had holy days (holidays) on the great feasts of Christmas and Easter.

Source C

Taken from a craftsman's calendar of holidays, for the year 1337. The craftsman was Roger Langele, a carpenter at the Tower of London.

Wednesday 1st January	Circumcision	Unpaid
Monday 6th January	Epiphany	Paid
Saturday 25th January	Conversion of St Paul	Unpaid
Saturday 22nd February	St Peter in the Cathedral	Paid
Monday 24th February	St Matthias	Unpaid
Tuesday 25th March	Annunciation of the Blessed Virgin Mary	Paid
Friday 18th April	Good Friday	Unpaid
Saturday 19th April	Eve of Easter	Paid

Why become a shrine?

People were very keen to have a relic of a saint in their church. Shines were very profitable.

Pilgrims brought offerings to shrines. They brought money and gold and silver images of the saint (or, if the saint was supposed to cure illness, of parts of the body that needed healing). All these things were left at the shrine.

Pilgrims often stayed at the shrine for several days. So they had to stay somewhere. If the shrine was in an abbey, the monks got to charge the pilgrims for food and a bed. They might sell pilgrims badges, too. If the shrine was in a city (like Thomas Becket's in Canterbury), the local townspeople got to make a profit out of the pilgrims in the same way.

Source D

Shepherds dancing at Christmas time. Taken from a manuscript made in the 15th century.

In 1132 a tremendous row broke out in York Abbey, which was one of the greatest **Benedictine** monasteries in England. Ranulf, Thomas, Gamel, Hamo, Walter, Gregory and Richard thought that their fellow **monks** had gone soft. York Abbey had grown rich and prosperous, and the monks were living a comfortable life. This was not at all what their founder, St. Benedict had said should happen.

Ranulf and his six supporters pressed the Abbot (Abbot Geoffrey) to make changes which would force the monks to lead a simpler life. Abbot Geoffrey could not decide what to do. He knew there were people, the **Cistercians**, who wanted to bring monks back to the simple, hard life laid down by St. Benedict. He didn't want any of that sort of trouble in his abbey! While he dithered, more monks joined Ranulf and his group.

Archbishop Thurstan got to hear about the problem. In October he visited the abbey to sort things out. As he arrived, a fight broke out in the **cloisters**.

Some of the monks were afraid the Archbishop would force change upon them. Archbishop Thurstan acted quickly. He put all the monks who wanted reform under his protection, and took them away to his palace in York. Archbishop Thurstan decided they should have their own monastery. He gave them some land in Skelldale on which to build their own abbey.

Source B

From the Rule of St. Benedict, who lived 480-543:

Idleness is the enemy of the soul. The brothers should have regular times for work and for reading prayers.
A mattress, woollen blanket and pillow is enough for bedding.
All monks should take turns to wait on each other so that no one is excused kitchen work.
Above all, care must be taken of the sick.

Source A

Monks singing at a service. Taken from a medieval manuscript.

Source C

From the *Fountains Chronicle* written by an eyewitness, Brother Hugh of Kirkstall, in about 1206. It is a description of Skelldale.

The land was thick with thorns, lying between the slopes of mountains and among rocks jutting out on both sides. It was more suitable as the home of wild beasts than the home of human beings.

Here the holy men gathered to seek shelter keeping off the harsh winter as best they could with straw and grasses thrown over them.
At night they usually sang psalms according to the Rule. By day they worked, some weaving mats, others taking withies [young trees] from a nearby wood to build a chapel, others cultivating gardens.

Source D

A modern reconstruction of Fountains Abbey. Here the artist, Alan Sorrell, has painted a picture of Fountains Abbey as he believed it would have looked in the 1400s.

Source E

A modern photograph of Fountains Abbey in North Yorkshire.

Archbishop Thurstan

Archbishop Thurstan was born in Normandy and became a monk at the abbey of Bayeux. Like many other monks, he worked in the government, too.

Thurstan built up more and more power, and was given more and more important jobs in the Church and in the government.

Thursan became archbishop of York in 1114. He kept this job until he died in 1140. He helped to set up Fountains Abbey and many other monasteries and nunneries. Thurstan also worked hard at extending his power. He pushed to have the Archbishopric of York made as important as that of Canterbury. He did not succeed.

The number of monks in Britain grew from about 1,000 in 1066 to around 13,000 by the end of the 1200s. By 1300 one person in every 200 was a monk. In addition to this, over 30,000 people worked for the monasteries as servants. The monks, and what they did, played an important part in the life of Britain.

You have already seen (on page 24) that monks prayed a lot and had to go to many services in the monastery chapel. But what else did they do? Look at the sources on this page and find out.

Source B

William of Malmesbury was a Benedictine monk. He wrote this about Cistercian monks, like the ones at Fountains Abbey, in about 1140:

Many of their rules are strict. They sleep with their clothes on. No one is allowed to miss prayers unless they are ill. From September to Easter they have only one meal a day, except on Sundays. They never go outside the monastery except to work, and they do not speak except to the Abbot.

Source A

One of the most important things monks did was to make beautiful books. Sometimes they copied old books, to make sure that ancient learning was not lost. Sometimes they wrote their own books. These might be accounts of their own time called **chronicles** or books about medicine and the treatments they used when caring for sick people. Monks usually **illuminated** their books with tiny paintings of birds and flowers.

Source C

From the account book of the monk who was Bursar (looked after the money) at Fountains Abbey. These are part of the expenses he paid out for entertaining the Duke of York in 1457:

To a servant of John de Markenfield, for bringing partridges	2d
Venison for the Abbot	10d
For fresh fish	2s 8d
To the servant of Agnes Sparth, of Ripon, for bringing shellfish	20d
For clavicords [like pianos]	2s
For repairing the clock	6s
For a paper map of the world	8d
For coals	7s 8d
To the minstrels of Beverley	16d
To the storyteller of the Earl of Salisbury	12d
To a fool from Byland	4d
To the actors of Ripon	2d

Source D

This painting of a **cellarer** comes from a thirteenth-century illuminated manuscript made by monks. **Cellarers** kept the keys to the wine cellar. Some monasteries were famous for making good wine.

Money from wool

The monks at Fountains were at first very poor. However, they worked hard at sheep-farming and gradually the wool they produced became famous all over Europe. They were soon running a successful woollen business and making a great deal of money!

On top of this, wealthy people gave money, silver and gold, and precious jewels to the Abbey hoping that this would get them to Heaven quickly. So the Abbey got richer and richer. The monks began to forget the Rule of St. Benedict and started to make their own lives more comfortable.

Source E

Written in about 1386 by an English poet, Geoffrey Chaucer in his poem, *The Canterbury Tales.*

A monk there was, one of the finest sort
Who rode the country; hunting was his sport.
A manly man, fit to be an Abbot.
He had many dainty horses in his stable.
The Rule of good St. Benedict
As old and strict he tended to ignore;
Greyhounds he had, as swift as birds, to run.
Hunting a hare or riding at a fence
Was all his fun, no matter what it cost.

Monks

There were many different sorts of monks. There were scholarly monks, learned men who read and wrote books. There were monks who also worked for the king, and spent a lot of time out in the world. They were the ones often seen as greedy and grasping.

At the opposite end of the scale, there were hermits. These were monks who shut themselves away, even from other monks, to devote themselves to praying. And, at the bottom of the heap, were the ordinary monks who spent their time praying and working for their abbey.

3.6 NUNS AND NUNNERIES

Christian women and girls who wanted to spend their lives serving God became nuns and lived in **nunneries**. There, they followed, more or less, the **Rule of St. Benedict** and did much the same sorts of things as monks in monasteries. However, there were far fewer nuns than monks. Between 1250 and 1540, 126-136 nunneries were set up, but only four had more than thirty women and sixty-three had fewer than ten. Why was this? Some women became nuns because they wanted to give their lives to God. Others became nuns because their only future was marriage, and they wanted to do something different.

Becoming a nun meant that a girl would be educated and she would learn about working in and running an organisation. She would have responsibilities that would be different, and perhaps more interesting, than being a wife and mother. This was, of course, only true of girls from wealthy families - and there weren't so many of these. Girls from poorer families had always been able to earn their own livings in workshops and on the land. Indeed, many of them had to. Their families couldn't afford to send them to nunneries, even if they had wanted to.

Source A

This painting of nuns in a nunnery was made in about 1300. In the top row, can you find the **sacristan** pulling the bell ropes? She was in charge of the church building and everything in it. The **abbess,** who in this picture is holding a **crozier,** was in charge of all the nuns in the nunnery. The **cellaress** is holding her keys to the wine cellar. In the bottom row, nuns are walking, and singing, in procession.

JULIAN OF NORWICH

Julian of Norwich is the name given to a religious woman who spent most of her life in a tiny shelter in the churchyard of St Julian's Church at Norwich. She was born about 1342 and probably began her life as a nun at Carrow, outside Norwich.

She was especially holy, and had many visions. One particular vision happened in 1373 when she thought she was dying. She said afterwards that she could feel her life ebbing away when suddenly she had a series of visions which seemed to come from a cross in her room. All her pain vanished and she lived for many more years.

She wrote about these visions. Her writings were later put together and called *Revelations of Divine Love*. One of the things she wrote was that: *All will be well and all will be well and all manner of things will be well*, which showed how much she trusted in God to bring about that which was right.

Less well off

Many nunneries were very poor. They were poor for different reasons. Nunneries in the north of England were often raided by Scotsmen from across the border. Other nunneries complained that they were always having to give meals to rich and powerful people, who didn't pay for them. Some nunneries were badly managed by nuns who had no experience of financial matters.

Lacock Abbey

Many nunneries helped their local communities. The nunnery at Lacock is a good example of this. It was founded in 1232 by Ela, Countess of Salisbury, after her husband died. People living in nearby villages became tenants of Lacock. Every year, on the anniversary of Ela's death, one hundred poor people were given bread and herrings. Ela was buried in the nunnery church. Two of her granddaughters joined the nunnery and kept up the family connection.

Outside influences

Some nunneries took in widows and wives for short periods as lodgers. This brought in money and kept the nuns in touch with the outside world. This wasn't always a good thing. Some nuns wanted to be fashionable. Some nunneries spent money on parties at New Year and Twelfth Night, on May Day games and bonfire nights, and on actors and plays at Christmas.

Clemthorpe nunnery

Clemthorpe was a town nunnery, about a mile outside the city of York. It was set up in about 1130 by Archbishop Thurstan. The nuns (usually about ten of them) ran a school and took in visitors who wanted to stay at the nunnery to rest. They also looked after sick people.

Source B

Nuns often acted as teachers, nurses and also looked after travellers. This medieval painting shows a nun and her pupils.

Source C

Eileen Power described what it was like in some nunneries by the end of the 1400s. She wrote this in *Medieval Women*, published in 1975.

Archbishops and bishops were shocked that nuns wore golden hairpins and silver belts, jewelled rings, laced shoes, slashed tunics, low-necked dresses, costly materials and furs. Bishops regarded pets as bad for discipline and tried to turn animals out. Nuns just waited until the bishops went and whistled the dogs back again. Dogs were easily the favourite pets, but nuns also kept monkeys, squirrels, rabbits and birds. They sometimes took animals to church with them.

Choosing a monarch

Nowadays there is a law which says who will inherit the throne when a monarch dies. The new monarch will be the eldest son of the dead king or queen. If there are no sons, the crown will go to the eldest daughter. It was different in medieval times. Sometimes the dying monarch decided who would rule after him; sometimes the king's sons quarrelled amongst themselves as to which of them should rule; sometimes the earls thought they should have a say. Sometimes, no matter how well a king had organised matters before his death, earls and other powerful people changed their minds afterwards, and backed different claimants.

What did it take to become a monarch?

In medieval times, a monarch had to be physically strong and have a strong personality. A monarch had to be physically strong because he had to travel around his kingdom on horseback. He would have to be able to lead his armies into battle, too. He needed a strong personality because he would have to control, and win the respect of, powerful earls. He had to give justice to everyone even if this upset strong and wealthy people. He had to keep control of the government, with no real centre to do it from and no parliament to make laws. Most people in medieval times believed monarchs had to be men.

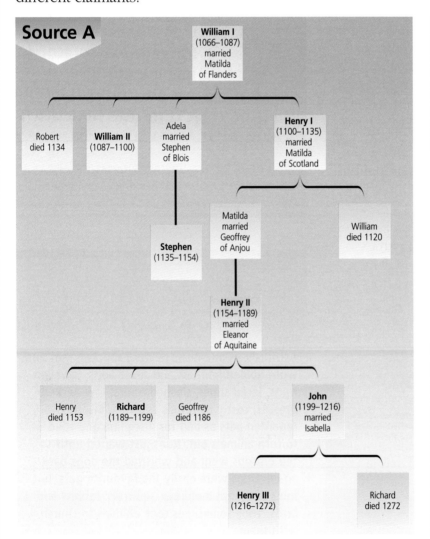

Source A

This is part of the family tree of the English kings between 1066 and 1272. The eldest child is on the left and the youngest on the right. The dates in brackets are the years they reigned.

Becoming king

The people in **bold** have been kings. William II became king after William I because Robert (his elder brother) died before William I. Henry I became king after William II because William had no sons.

MATILDA V. STEPHEN

In November 1120 the *White Ship* was crossing the Channel from Normandy to England. On board were about 300 earls, their wives and sons – and William, the only **legitimate** son of King Henry I. The sea was calm, the moon and stars were bright, and the visit to Normandy had been successful. Everyone got very drunk. The barons persuaded the ship's captain to race the other ships in the little fleet. Suddenly there was a tremendous crash and a grinding of timbers on rock. The *White Ship* sank quickly. There was only one survivor – a butcher.

Henry was distraught. Not only was his son dead, but there was only a girl – his daughter Matilda – to succeed him. Henry did what he could to make sure Matilda inherited the throne when he died. He made the most powerful earls in the land swear that they would support her as their Queen. Henry died in 1135. Immediately, many of the earls who had promised to support Matilda changed their minds. Matilda was bossy and determined. They didn't want a woman monarch – and besides, she was married to Geoffrey of Anjou. He was French and would reign with her. They thought he would try to take over the country. The earls switched their support to Count Stephen, Henry's nephew. He was crowned before Matilda could even get to England.

Matilda was furious, and so were the earls who remained loyal to her. They gathered together an army to fight Stephen and his supporters. The result was a bloody civil war. A **chronicler** wrote *All England was aflame*. Matilda very nearly won. For four years she had Stephen imprisoned and ruled by herself. Finally the war ended. Matilda agreed to give up her claim to the throne provided her son Henry became king on Stephen's death.

Source B

From *The Anglo-Saxon Chronicle* 1137. The chronicler is describing England under Stephen's rule.

The earls filled the country full of castles and used them against the King. They forced the unhappy people of the country to work on the castles. They raised taxes on the villages.

When the wretched people had no more to give, they robbed and burned all the villages, so that you could easily go for a whole day's journey and never find anyone in a village, or land being farmed. Corn, meat, butter and cheese were expensive, because there was none in the country.

Women rulers

Medieval people thought that women were not fit to rule. There were several reasons for this:

- Women were seen as less able to think clearly.

- Medieval monarchs often had to fight. Women were not supposed to fight.

- Women were expected to marry. Marriage to a foreign prince would make a foreigner king of England.

Henry II ruled over a vast empire, as you can see from the map. His mother, Matilda, died in 1150 and he inherited Normandy from her. The following year he inherited Anjou from his father. In 1152, Henry married Eleanor of Aquitaine, and added her lands to his empire in France. Finally, when Stephen died in 1154, Henry gained England. He made the headquarters of his government at the Palace of Westminster in London.

Henry thought it important that he saw for himself what was happening in his empire. He was a tireless traveller. In the thirty-two years of his reign he crossed the English Channel twenty-eight times and spent Christmas in twenty-four different places.

Henry became King of England in 1154. He immediately set about putting right the problems created by the civil war between Stephen and Matilda. He did this by:

- ordering every castle built in Stephen's reign to be destroyed

- sending foreign knights home

- taking back Royal lands given by Stephen to earls in order to gain their support

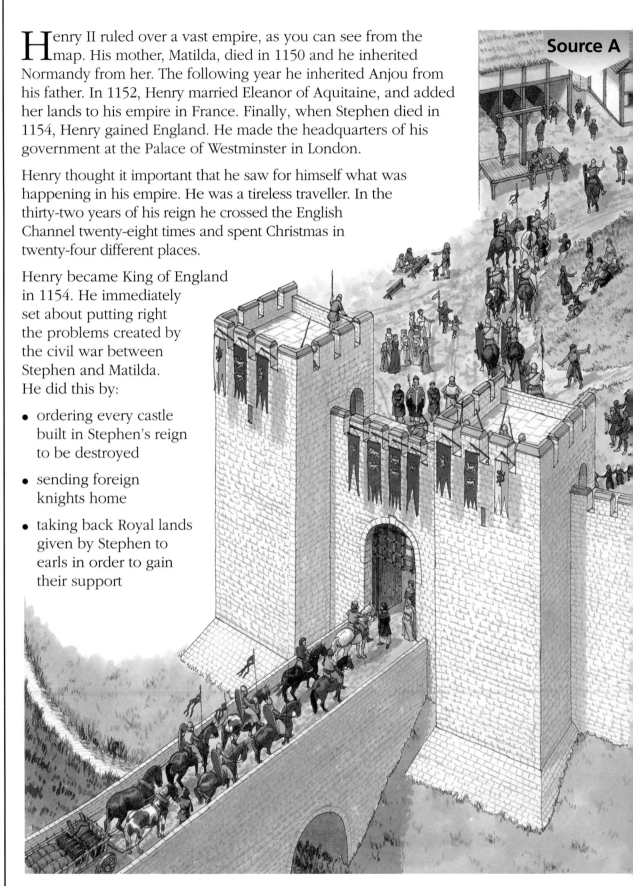

Source A

- encouraging earls to pay him a fee instead of providing knights. This meant that the number of fighting men was cut back, and Henry had the cash to hire soldiers when and wherever he needed them. Until this point, English kings had relied on the earls to provide him with an army of knights. The king would call on these knights whenever he needed them. Because more fighting was taking place in France, the king no longer needed an English army at the ready.

A new system of justice

Henry also reformed the system of royal justice. England had long been divided into **shires** and into smaller units called **hundreds**. Henry appointed sheriffs and travelling judges to the shire and hundred courts, and often acted as a judge himself. The taxes that were collected went straight into the **exchequer**. In these ways Henry kept firm control of the legal system.

Under Henry's rule, England and the rest of the Angevin Empire grew strong and prospered.

Henry II, his officials, soldiers and followers ride back to Orford Castle, in Suffolk. There the King is to judge accused people at one of his courts.

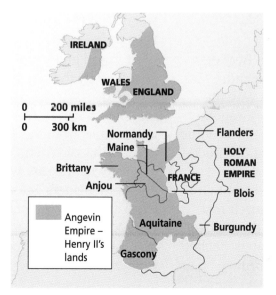

The Angevin Empire in the twelfth century.

Peter Blois

Peter Blois was a churchman who worked for kings all over Europe. He was Henry II's private secretary. Because he had trained in law, he helped to sort out legal tangles.

He did not always do this honestly. Papers left behind from the time show that he changed evidence, probably for a bribe! Peter went on the First Crusade and wrote about it. He also wrote other short books on history.

4.3 CHURCH V. STATE: THE MURDER OF AN ARCHBISHOP IN 1170

On 29 December 1170, four dusty, tired and angry knights rode into Canterbury. They forced their way into Archbishop Thomas Becket's palace. The monks were afraid that the knights would harm Becket. They hustled him into the cathedral. They thought no-one would draw a sword in such a holy place. But the knights followed. They killed Becket in front of the altar. They sliced through his skull and his blood and brains splattered over the floor of the cathedral. The knights believed that murdering Becket would please the King, Henry II. Why did they think this?

Church and State

As you have seen on page 20, the Pope ran the Christian Church. But kings wanted to control everything in their own kingdoms, including Church matters. Henry II wanted one system of justice in England. Priests, and anyone who worked for the Church, could be tried by a special Church court if they were accused of doing anything wrong. Church court punishments were usually much lighter than those in the King's courts. Henry wanted to limit the power of Church courts. The Archbishop of Canterbury, the most important churchman in England, had to be someone he could trust to agree with him.

A new archbishop

Henry decided to make Thomas Becket, his friend and Chancellor of England, Archbishop of Canterbury. That way the Church and the State would work together. Becket wasn't a priest but he could become one – and then become Archbishop. Becket refused. He warned Henry that if he became a priest he would have to put God and the rules of the Catholic Church first. Henry didn't listen. He insisted that Becket did as he was told. In 1162 Thomas Becket became Archbishop of Canterbury.

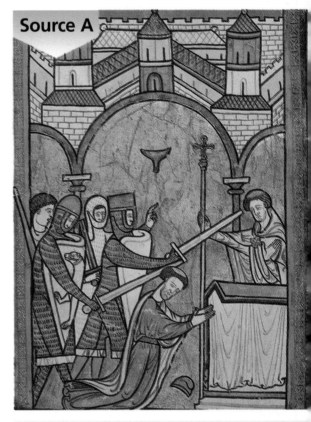

Source A

This picture of the murder of Thomas Becket was painted in about 1200. The priest on the right is Edward Grim. He wrote down what happened. In Source B you can read part of what he wrote.

Quarrels break out

Henry and Becket soon quarrelled. In 1164 Henry made a law saying churchmen who were found guilty in Church courts had to be punished by the King's courts. Becket told the clergy not to obey this new law. He said the Church had to run its own affairs without interference from the King. Henry was angry because his old friend would not work with him for what he saw was the good of the kingdom. Matters got so bad that Becket had to go and live in France. Finally, in 1170 Becket and Henry patched up their quarrel and Henry allowed Becket to return home from exile.

Yet more trouble

Once back in Canterbury, Becket promptly excommunicated (banished from the church) the bishops who had sided with Henry. Henry was in Normandy when he was told what Becket had done. He was furious and is supposed to have raged: *Who will rid me of this turbulent priest?* Four knights, hoping to please the king, slipped away. They were going to kill the Archbishop.

Was Henry pleased?

When Henry heard what they had done he was beside himself with grief and rage. No matter what he had said in anger, he had never intended this to happen.

In 1174 he went to Canterbury. He was going to show his sorrow at Becket's murder and at his part in it. Henry walked barefoot through the streets to Thomas Becket's tomb. He walked slowly, and bishops whipped his back as he went. Henry, the most powerful king in Europe, was showing his repentance. In doing so he ended the long quarrel with the Church.

Source B

From the eyewitness account of Edward Grim, written in the early 1170s.

The murderers came in full armour with swords and axes. The monks begged the Archbishop to flee to the Cathedral. But he refused. He had wanted to be a martyr [someone who dies for their cause] for a long time. However, the monks seized him and pushed him into the church. The four knights followed. The Archbishop ordered the doors of the cathedral to be kept open.

They tried to drag the Archbishop out of the cathedral. But Thomas clung on to a pillar and would not let go. One of the knights, Reginald Fitzurse, cut him on the top of his head. By the same stroke he almost cut off my arm. For, when the monks ran away, I stood by the Archbishop and put my arms round him to protect him. He stood firm to a second blow on the head. At the third blow he fell to his knees, whispering 'For the name of Jesus and the protection of the Church I am ready to die'. Roger Brito gave him a terrible blow as he lay on the floor. Hugh Mauclerc put his foot on Becket's neck. He scattered blood and brains across the floor shouting to the others 'Let us go. This fellow will not be getting up again'.

Edward Grim

Edward Grim was a monk from Cambridge who went to visit Thomas Becket when he returned to England in 1170. He had never met the Archbishop before. Despite this, it was Grim who defended Becket when he was attacked in Canterbury Cathedral.

Grim defended Becket until he was badly wounded, when he managed to drag himself to the shelter of the altar. Grim's story of the murder must have been written after 1174, because it describes the penance that Henry II made in Canterbury in that year.

Outcomes

The people of Canterbury, when they heard of Becket's murder, rushed to the cathedral to collect what they could of his blood. They believed it would perform miracles.

In 1173 the Pope made Thomas Becket a saint.

Ever since 1170, people have made pilgrimages to Thomas Becket's tomb in Canterbury cathedral.

Church courts continued to punish churchmen accused of crimes.

The King continued to appoint bishops and archbishops.

4.4 CROWN V. BARONS: KING JOHN AND MAGNA CARTA 1215

King Henry II, as you have seen, ruled over the vast Angevin Empire. He kept a tight hold on the English earls. Under Henry, England and the rest of the Angevin Empire grew strong and wealthy.

King Henry's younger son, John, became king in 1199. For John, disaster seemed to follow disaster.

- By 1204 John had lost Normandy, Anjou, Maine and Touraine to the invading armies of the clever and skilful French king, Philip.
- In 1205, John quarrelled with the Pope as to who should be the next Archbishop of Canterbury. Kings and popes often quarrelled, as you have seen. However, this quarrel was particularly bad. In 1208 the Pope put all England under an **interdict.** This meant that priests were forbidden to take any church services. The churches were closed. The interdict lasted until 1213, when John gave in to the Pope because he wanted his help against the English barons.

- In 1215 many barons rebelled against John. For eleven years John had been trying desperately to win back his lands in France. He taxed ordinary people and he taxed the barons in order to pay for his wars against the French king. Finally, the barons had had enough. They formed an army and took over London.

King John agreed to meet the barons. He said he would meet them at Runneymede, near the river Thames and Windsor Castle. The barons complained that John's taxes were unfair, and that those who could not pay were harshly punished and had no means of complaining. They wanted him to sign a **charter** (a sort of contract), promising to rule fairly. John took four days to make up his mind. Finally, on 19 June 1215, he agreed to the Great Charter – the Magna Carta.

This picture of King John putting his seal to the Magna Carta was painted in the nineteenth century. You can see it today in the House of Commons in London.

Source A

King John, of course, had no intention of keeping to the promises he made when he put his seal on the Magna Carta. He had already got the Pope to agree to him breaking these promises because they had been made under threat. Not surprisingly, the barons did not trust John. Civil war broke out again.

Suddenly, however, in 1216 John became ill and died in the middle of a terrible storm. The new king, John's son Henry, was only nine years old. William Marshal, the Earl of Pembroke, ruled for him. One of the first things he did was to re-issue the Magna Carta in the name of the new king, Henry III.

What did the Magna Carta say?

Magna Carta was mainly to protect the rights of barons and knights, but it did protect ordinary people too. These are some of the most important of the sixty-three sections in the Charter:

- No scutage [tax] can be imposed on the barons unless they agree first.

- A man cannot be put on trial unless there are believable witnesses to accuse him.

- No free man can be seized or imprisoned, or stripped of his rights or possessions, or outlawed or exiled except by the law of the land.

- Justice will not be refused to anyone, nor will it be delayed nor sold.

- All merchants shall be free to buy and sell goods in England without extra charges.

- The barons shall elect twenty-five of their members to make sure that this Charter is obeyed.

Source A

Source A was painted about 700 years after the Magna Carta was signed. The artist has looked at pictures from the time to make his painting as realistic as possible.

Even so, we have to remember two things. Firstly, he was painting a picture to sell it. He had to make it look dramatic. Secondly, when the picture was painted the Magna Carta was thought of as a good thing. King John was even referred to in some history books as 'a bad man'! You can tell whose side the artist was on by looking at how he has painted the people.

ELEANOR OF AQUITAINE (1122–1204)

Eleanor of Aquitaine was a determined and forceful woman. She married Louis VII of France in 1137 and they had two daughters. While she was still his wife she is said to have led her own troops in the Second Crusade (1147–9) dressed as an Amazonian warrior! It was at this point that Louis' love for her began to fade. He had the marriage **annulled** (cancelled) in 1152.

Eleanor promptly married Henry, Count of Anjou, who became Henry II of England in 1154. Eleanor's lands of Aquitaine, which she had inherited from her father, were added to Henry's vast Angevin Empire. Eleanor and Henry had five sons and three daughters. Henry wasn't a particularly faithful husband. Not many monarchs were at that time. Eleanor, however, wasn't prepared to put up with this sort of behaviour in her husband.

When two of her sons, Richard and John, rebelled against their father, she supported them. Henry put her in prison in 1174. She wasn't released until 1189 when her eldest son, Richard, was King of England.

Eleanor helped rule England when Richard was off on his Crusades (1189–94) and raised money for his **ransom.** In 1200 there was a rebellion in Anjou against her second son, King John. Eleanor, by then over seventy years old, led the army that put down the rebels. She died four years later.

*Y*our path will be narrow, full of death and terrible with dangers. If you are captured you will face torture, chains and every possible suffering, warned Pope Urban II when he asked people to go on the First Crusade in 1095. Yet by 1096 thousands of people had left Europe to face these dangers and more. What was a crusade? Why did people go on them?

A holy war

The crusades were a series of wars where Christians and Muslims fought to control the 'Holy Land'. Jerusalem is a holy place for Christians because many important events in the life of Christ happened there. It is holy to the Muslim religion, Islam, too. Muslims believe their prophet, Muhammad, visited Heaven from there.

The First Crusade

The First Crusade began in 1096. In 1087 the Turks, who were Muslims, had taken over much of the Holy Land, including Jerusalem. The ruler of the Christian kingdom of Byzantium feared attack. He asked the Pope to raise an army from the rest of Christendom. He probably expected a few hundred lords. But Pope Urban II was persuasive. He toured Christendom, promising Heaven, land and loot to people who went on crusades. They flocked in – not just soldiers but ordinary people, sometimes whole families, spurred on by greed, religious feeling or both.

A lost cause?

The Muslim leader, Saladin, wrote to a Christian ruler at the start of the Third Crusade in 1189, warning: *There are more, many more of us than of you. Also, there is an ocean between you and any help you could call on. We have friends far closer. You have come against us twice before. But on both occasions you went back again.*

Saladin made a good point. The crusades were doomed from the start. The Holy Land was foreign to Christians. The weather, the food, the way of life were all different. The only way for Christians to settle was to behave like locals, and very few of them wanted to do this. So they went home. The Muslims were still there.

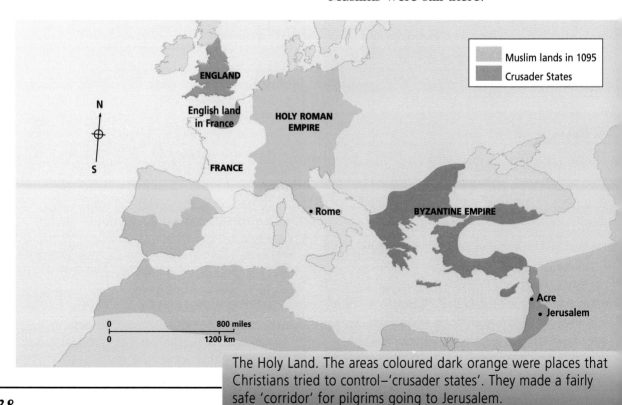

Muslim lands in 1095

Crusader States

The Holy Land. The areas coloured dark orange were places that Christians tried to control–'crusader states'. They made a fairly safe 'corridor' for pilgrims going to Jerusalem.

Some reasons for going on a crusade.

Different crusades?

The crusades dragged on and off for about 200 years. In some ways those who went on the First Crusade were the worst off. They had no real idea of the dangers—the physical dangers of the journey, the weather or the enemy (many people expected the Turks would run away when they saw the crusaders). Later crusaders were better prepared. But in other ways almost every crusade was the same. The Christian kings always squabbled among themselves. There was always heat, danger, disease and homesickness.

Stephen of Blois

Stephen of Blois married William I's daughter, Adela. She made him go on the First Crusade. He wrote home: *We have endured sufferings and evils without number. Many have already spent all they have and rely on God and charity. It is excessively cold and enormously wet.*

These pages look at the lives, and deaths, of some of the crusaders at the siege of Acre, during the Third Crusade. This was one of the longest sieges ever. People both inside and outside the city suffered terribly. Most of the quotes on these pages come from a history of the Third Crusade written by a monk in around 1200 from the memories of a knight who was there.

Conditions for ordinary soldiers

By October 1190 conditions outside the city were as bad as inside:

Food shortages came to a crisis. All the soldiers were tormented by ceaseless hunger. Winter was not far off. This had once been a time of easy living, but times had changed. Stomachs that had rumbled through being too full, now growled with hunger. All our supplies were used up and the troops were still hungry. The hot weather made things worse. Even well-brought-up lords would fling themselves to the ground to chew at plants that they saw growing.

Priceless horses were killed and eaten, sometimes without even skinning them. Some were so desperate with hunger that they would chew and lick bones, even if they had been chewed by dogs for days before. They got no goodness from it, but maybe had the pleasure of chewing at the memory of meat.

One of the earliest pictures of the Siege of Acre, painted in 1280. The Crusaders wore chain-mail and helmets, to protect them from arrows and spears. But this armour was heavy and difficult to move in quickly. It also made the people wearing it very hot. Many knights sold (or even threw away) their armour during the long march to the Holy Land.

RICHARD I (1157–99)

Richard I, King of England, was called 'the Lionheart' because of his courage. He got this nick-name (so the story goes) by ripping out and eating the heart of a lion.

Richard's arrival at Acre, in June 1191, was the turning point in the siege:

Richard and his troops landed at Acre, and everyone rejoiced. People were so glad that he had arrived that they played pipes, trumpets and drums. They sang and got very drunk. They lit so many torches that the Turks in the city must have thought that the whole valley was on fire.

Richard's fleet stopped supplies getting to the city. Thirty-four days after Richard arrived the Turks surrendered and the Crusaders marched into Acre. Almost at once, they began to squabble about how to divide the loot.

Source A

This picture, painted in about 1280, shows women besieging their enemies.

Women crusaders

At the start of the Third Crusade King Henry II's rules said there should be no women on the crusades, except, perhaps, washerwomen. But by the time the crusaders reached Acre there were women with them. At least some of these women were wives who had gone believing in the crusaders' cause. These women faced the dangers of the crusades on equal terms with their men, as the following story shows:

AN UNNAMED HEROINE

Among those carrying soil to fill the ditch around the city was a woman who worked very hard. A Turk struck her a fatal blow with a spear. She fell to the ground and lay there in agony. Her husband hurried to her side. 'My love,' she said, 'I beg you, don't let my body – for I shall soon be dead – be moved. Let my corpse lie in the ditch in place of a load of earth, it will be earth soon anyway.'

The washerwomen of Acre

The crusaders had collected quite a group of washerwomen by the time they reached Acre. It is hard to imagine the difficulties of their job, dealing with the clothes of very hot and sweaty crusaders, even finding water to wash them in. They probably used seawater. The Muslim writer Baha' ad Din was fascinated by the washerwomen. He said they came *to keep the crusaders' linen clean, to wash their hair and to catch the lice on them, which they did as skilfully as monkeys. Everywhere was full of old women. They urged the crusaders on in battle, shouting that it would be glorious for them to die for their God.* If the Muslims captured any of these women by accident they sent them straight back to the crusaders.

The squabble for Acre

The squabble between Christian monarchs over Acre was made worse by the merchants of Pisa and Genoa, who wanted to be the only ones to trade from Acre. They took sides too.

Stories about England in King Richard's reign (like the Robin Hood stories) suggest the biggest effect of the Third Crusade on England was that the King was not there. They show Richard as a strong, wise man, who loved England and the English. They show his brother John treating everyone badly. Is this true? What effect did the Third Crusade have on England?

An absent king

The Third Crusade cost England a lot of money. Despite this, Richard was a popular king. He spent just five months of his reign in England and could hardly speak any English, but he had about him an air of glamour: he was a good poet as well as a brave fighter. He liked feasting and tournaments. But most importantly, he could control the English lords. So the country was at peace with him in charge. When he went to the Third Crusade he left some of the most powerful lords, including his brother John, to run the country. They taxed people heavily. They also fought among themselves.

Captured!

In 1192 Richard was captured on his way home and handed over to Henry VI of Germany – one of the many people he had quarrelled with. While he waited for a huge ransom to be paid, King Louis of France helped himself to huge chunks of Richard's French lands.

Family losses

A lot of people died on the Third Crusade. Many of the most important families in the country had sent at least one son to fight. Many of them never came back. Histories written at the time give long lists of people from important families all over Europe who were killed. Many more ordinary people would have been killed, but their deaths are not recorded.

Richard I and Philip at Gisors

When Richard's ransom was paid he came straight back to England. He stayed just long enough to stop the lords fighting and have himself crowned as King for the second time to make the point that he was in charge. Then he went off to France to re-capture the land there lost to Louis of France. He was killed in battle in 1199.

Source A

High taxes

Henry II had demanded high taxes to set up the Third Crusade. Taxes stayed high all through Richard's reign and, despite the fighting between the lords, seem to have been efficiently collected. When Richard was taken prisoner, his captor set a huge ransom demand. The English paid, mostly with money raised by taxes.

Were there any good effects?

The crusaders were not fighting with the Muslims all the time. In times of relative peace Christians in the crusader states, Spain and Sicily, got to know the Muslims better. Some of them saw there were good things about the Muslim way of life. They even traded with each other.

Forbidden contact

The kings of the various Christian countries tried to stop Christians mixing with Muslims. They made strict rules about not marrying or trading with Muslims. Some people obeyed these rules, others did not.

What did they learn?

Some of the things the crusaders learned from mixing with the Muslims were:

- Arabic numbers (the numbers we use now)
- the benefits of soap and regular baths
- the benefits of eating fresh food
- better ways of building, especially castles.

A Muslim doctor described a visit to a Christian camp in about 1150:
*They took me to see a knight with a boil on his leg. I put a **poultice** on the leg, and the boil began to heal. Then a French doctor came and said I had no idea how to treat the boil. He sent for a strong man and an axe. He put the knight's leg on a block of wood and said to the strong man, "strike hard and cleanly". The marrow spurted out of the bone when it was cut. The knight died at once.*

Source B

Muslim doctors were more respected by their patients than European doctors were. They often ran schools and taught religion too, so they were seen as professional people. Fewer of their patients died than those of European doctors. They knew more about drugs and hygiene.

Albucasis

Albucasis was a Muslim doctor who lived and worked in Spain in about 950, when it was ruled by Muslims. He wrote about surgery. He advised doctors not to operate unless they had to, and to observe the patient closely to work out what to do. English surgeons were not so careful.

Medieval villages were usually built near a lord's manor house. The lord controlled all the land. Most villagers were **villeins** – people who had to work on the lord's land, and could not move away. A few were free men who paid rent in money, not work. Everyone worked in the fields most of the time. This sounds as if all villages were the same. They were not. They varied greatly in size. The land and weather affected the size of villages and how they grew.

The land and weather

The land and weather affected what people grew and the animals they kept. Some land was bad for growing crops. Woods were hard to clear. Moorland was too high, windy and cold. Marshland was too wet and boggy. Even land that could grow crops varied. Heavy clay soil was harder to plough than light sandy soil. Clay and sandy soil both grew less food in the same space than rich soil. The best land was where people could grow crops and keep animals.

It made sense for villagers to use the land for what it did best. Villagers with good growing land used as much as they could of it to grow food. They bought wood from elsewhere and kept very few animals, or sent their animals somewhere else to graze.

Cuxham

We are going to take a close look at one village, Cuxham, in 1315. Cuxham is in Oxfordshire, on good farming land, at the edge of the Chilterns, which were mostly woodland. Cuxham people were able to grow crops and keep animals. Cuxham did not have a lord of the manor in 1315. The lands were held by Merton College, Oxford, instead. But the College did the same things that a lord would have done. We know about Cuxham because the College kept lots of records, which are still there today.

The pictures

Most of the pictures in this part of the book come from a book called *The Luttrell Psalter*, made in about 1320.

The church

Cuxham church had a house for the priest to live in, with land attached to it. The priest also had strips of land in the fields. In 1315 the priest did not live in Cuxham. He paid a chaplain to do his duties instead.

The chaplain collected the tithes (see page 21), not only from the villagers but also from the College, even down to one tenth of the apples in the orchard. He held church services and baptised, married and buried the villagers.

The miller was an important person in Cuxham. All the villagers had to use him to grind their wheat and barley at his mill and paid him a fee.

Source A

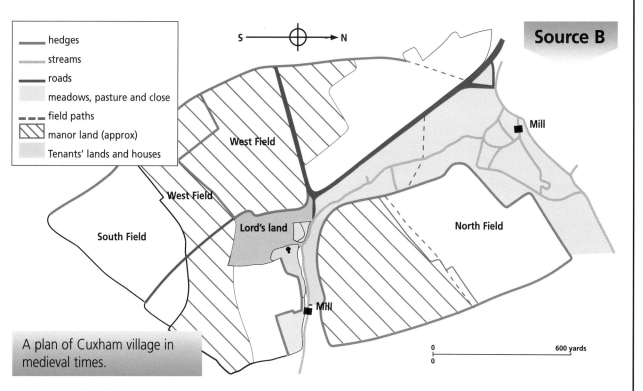

Legend:
- hedges
- streams
- roads
- meadows, pasture and close
- field paths
- manor land (approx)
- Tenants' lands and houses

S — N

West Field

West Field

South Field

Lord's land

North Field

Mill

Mill

A plan of Cuxham village in medieval times.

0 — 600 yards
0

Farming the land

The villagers grew crops in three big fields. One field grew a mix of oats, barley, peas and beans and vetch (vetch was fed to animals). The next grew wheat. The last field was left to rest, so the soil did not lose its goodness through constant use. Each field was used for each crop in turn. These three fields were used by the lord, the priest and the villeins. The lord took a large piece of land out of each field. The rest was farmed by the priest and the villeins in strips. Each person had several strips in each field.

The village mills

The village had three mills:
- Cutt Mill was the College mill. The villagers had to pay to grind their wheat and barley there. The mill was rented at £2 a year, with a two-roomed house and land. Robert Oldman was the miller.
- A mill at the east end of the village. It was rented out at about 10s a year.
- The fulling mill. The fuller washed woollen cloth and beat it to clean it and thicken it up. The mill was built in about 1312. It was rented to the fuller, Robert Digger, with a two-roomed house and land, at about 13s a year. This mill is not marked on the map because there is no evidence about where it was.

Dividing the strips

Villagers marked the edges of their strip with chunks of chalk or rock as markers. There were also paths trodden between the strips. Each year the markers were checked. People did move the marker stones from time to time, to try to get a bit more land in their strip.

The mill

The mill (just like most of the other houses in Cuxham) was a wooden-framed building with mud (daub) walls and a thatched roof.

The doors and window shutters were made from wood, with iron locks and hinges.

We have seen that most medieval villages had a lord and a priest. They were the most important people in the village. But what about the villagers? What were they like?

ROBERT OLDMAN THE REEVE

Cuxham's reeve was the miller, Robert Oldman. He and his wife, Agnes, had at least three sons and maybe a daughter. Robert took advantage of his job in small ways. He took more than his share of malted barley (the main ingredient in beer) from the College's crop. Robert brewed most of the beer in the village. He also kept his pigs on College land. We know this because the College found out and fined him. But the College kept him in the job from 1311 until his death in 1349, so they must have been happy with the way he ran things.

Robert probably felt entitled to cheat a bit, because the job had inconveniences as well as advantages. The College expected him to use his own horse and cart for College business. They sent him on errands to local towns. In 1313 he had a dreadful trip to Abingdon (about 16km away) to buy an ox. He spent the night at Dorchester (about halfway home). That night the ox got loose. Robert found it two days later, at Filkins, about 40km from home!

The reeve

The reeve ran things for the lord. He said what to plant, and when. He organised work, like harvesting, which involved the whole village. He hired extra people at busy times. He sold spare crops, ran the lord's own land and made sure everyone did their jobs. If the strips of land the villeins farmed were changed, he decided who got which strips.

Reeve or bailiff?

Manors with no lord living there were looked after by a reeve or a bailiff. Reeves were local tenants. They were part of the village. Bailiffs were not. They were brought in from outside, and often moved into the manor house. Reeves might use the manor land, but tended to stay in their own homes.

Source A

Villeins

Villeins agreed to work for the lord in return for a house, garden and land of their own in the big fields. Agreements were usually for the life of the villein. Anyone who took on the land when he died, even his wife, had to give the lord their best animal as a fee. Villeins had to work on the lord's land for a number of days yearly, and could not leave the village.

Cuxham's villeins usually worked 2 days a week, more at harvest time. This was the same as many villages, but some lords drove a hard bargain, making people work for three or even four days a week.

Cottagers

Cottagers had to work on the lord's land and promise not to leave the village, just like the villeins. Their agreements were usually for the life of the cottager, too. Anyone taking over their land had to give their best animal, too. But because they only had a house and garden, not strips in the open fields, they had to work fewer days. Villagers could hold land as cottagers and villeins at the same time, if they did two lots of work.

Cuxham cottagers worked just 6 days a year for the lord, mostly at harvest time. This was the same as many other villages.

JOAN OVERCHURCH, VILLEIN AND COTTAGER

Joan Overchurch and her husband John were cottagers with 6 extra acres of field strips for which they were supposed to work 1 day a week and more at harvest. Instead they paid 2s 6d a year rent. Villeins and cottagers could pay rent instead of working, or pay someone to do the work for them. By 1309 they also had the villein land held by John's brother Richard, who died.

Late in 1311 John died. Soon after, Joan's house burned down. The fire left Joan in a bad way. The College said she did not have to give them an animal for the land – her only animal had died in the fire. They also let her off a year's rent, and gave her some wheat and barley to keep her going. Joan passed all the land on to her son Elias and moved to the cottager land.

JOHN GREEN THE FREEMAN

John Green and his father Robert were the only freemen in the village. They rented land in Cuxham and the nearby villages, adding to it bit by bit. They then rented out most of their land for more money. They got steadily richer.

By 1315 John had an ox and at least 50 sheep, as well as farming land. John and his wife Matilda Freeland had at least three sons, John, Thomas and Hugh. They were about twice as rich as Robert Oldman, the best-off villein.

Harvest time was one of the busiest times of the year. The whole village was out in the fields working and extra workers were hired in. These two pictures of harvest time come from a 14th century manuscript.

Freemen

Freemen rented their land from the lord of the manor. They did not have to work on the lord's land. They could move around as they wanted.

The fishpond

This was used to keep fish for the use of the College and any visitors. The pond had roach, bream and pike. It was also used as a duckpond. This did not always work well. Ducklings were sometimes eaten by the bigger fish!

Who worked there?

All the time:

- 4 ploughmen, 2 holders (to hold the animals) and 2 drivers (to steer the animals) who work in the fields. The drivers may have been relatives of the slaves in the Domesday Survey of Cuxham.
- a carter
- a cowman and a dairy assistant (could be a man)
- a shepherd, helped by a boy hired in when the sheep had their lambs twice a year
- a gardener who looked after the vegetable plots and the orchards.

These people probably slept in the rooms over the main gate and next to the kitchen.

Part-time, as needed:

- a woman to malt the barley
- a pig keeper, who looked after the villagers' pigs too.
- labourers hired in at busy times, mainly harvest
- a blacksmith
- builders (carpenters, masons and thatchers).

The barns

There were lots of barns. They were used to store wheat, barley, hay, straw, oats, peas and beans. The yard in front of the barns was used for jobs like threshing wheat and barley – hitting it to separate the grains from the stalks.

The lord's house

The rooms on the ground floor were used for storage. The first floor rooms (reached from outside by the staircase) were the living rooms. The lavatory was built out over the stream which ran from the springs in the orchard down through the fishponds to the village stream.

What happened to the crops?

Crops grown in the College share of the village fields:

- Wheat: about half sold, some saved to start next year, the rest sent to the College or given out as part of the wages.
- Barley: some sold, some kept for seed, most malted to make beer in the oven by the field.
- Oats: very little sold, some kept for seed, at least half fed to the animals.

Crops grown on the manor farm:

- Apples: sold as fruit and cider
- Vegetables: mostly eaten by manor workers or sent to the College.

The oven

The manor farm had an oven in the garden (in the bottom right of the picture). It was made of iron and covered in grass turf. The oven was probably used for malting barley. The barley was laid on woven twig trays, which were stacked in the oven so hot air could move around them.

What was life like in Cuxham in 1315? What did the villagers do? This depended on the time of year – how many hours of daylight they had to work out of doors and what jobs had to be done.

Working in the fields

The villagers got up at sunrise. After a breakfast of bread and beer, most of them went to work in the fields. They all had to do some jobs; spring ploughing and sowing, summer harvest. They had to plough or harvest the College fields before they did their own. They had to be quick, or their own would be harvested late. So the whole village, men, women and children, did these jobs. At other times people did different jobs. The men worked on the land. Women did some farm work but more often they stayed at home, looking after animals and children, the house and garden, cooking, brewing and spinning.

The villagers took their midday meal to the fields: bread and beer with cheese or even bacon or cold meat if they had any. They worked until dark. Then they went back to the village for supper. Supper was usually a stew of whatever vegetables they had growing in their garden, with more bread and beer. They often went to bed straight after supper.

Other work

Villagers did other work too. They had a shepherd and a pig keeper to look after the sheep and pigs. But they had to make and mend tools, clear ditches, mend walls, even repair their houses. In any spare time they had they did things to try to make money. Some people brewed beer or cider to sell, others spun wool to make cloth or carved bowls.

Daily bread

The villagers of Cuxham ate a lot of bread and drank a lot of beer. People drank less water in medieval times because it was dirty. The bread was made from the barley, or wheat (or both) they grew, made into flour at the College mill. The beer was more watery than beer today. Many families brewed their own beer, but three of the villagers made beer to sell as well. Robert Oldman made most beer, and so most money selling it.

Bread and beer were part of every meal. Villagers who had hens, cows or pigs also had eggs, milk and cheese and meat for at least part of the year.

Some villagers at work. They are carding (brushing wool to straighten the fibres) and spinning wool and weeding thistles from a field.

Source A

All work and no play?

The villagers worked all day. Once the sun went down it was dark outside, only the moon lit the village. They had to be indoors and had no space to get together. Did they ever have time off to enjoy themselves? Yes, they did. They were not allowed to work on Sunday. The College also gave them some holy days off.

What did they do with their time off? On Sundays and holy days they had to go to church at least once. Some work had to be done. Animals had to be fed, some had to be milked. Meals had to be made. Sometimes it was hard to tell what was work and what was not. If a man enjoyed carving spoons could he do this on Sunday, or was it work? Holy days were times for eating, dancing and singing. Some days had special events. On St. George's Day many villages acted out the story of George and the Dragon. On Midsummer's Day they stayed outdoors for a huge bonfire when it got dark.

What about the children?

Babies were swaddled (wrapped tightly in cloth strips, see the picture) which made them sleep a lot. Their mothers took them to work and hung them on a hook or a branch. Toddlers were harder to control. They were given simple jobs, like picking stones from the fields, as soon as they could walk. But they did wander off, and it could be dangerous. Young children drowned from falling into rivers, ditches or ponds. Village children did not go to school. Boys worked on the land, getting harder jobs as they got older and stronger. Girls worked on the land, and learned women's skills too, like spinning.

The village year

Spring:
Plough ground, clear stones.
Sow barley, oats and wheat.
Put animals out to grass.
Shear sheep.

Summer:
Harvest time.
Animals graze the stubble.
Pick fruit.

Autumn:
Thresh barley and wheat as needed. Plough ground, clear stones. Sow winter wheat, barley. Store hay for fodder. Kill pigs and other animals that cannot be fed through the winter. Hang the meat in the chimney to smoke it or put it in barrels with salt.

Winter:
Mend tools.
Mend fences and buildings.
Move animals into barns.

All year:
Brew beer, make cheese, spin wool, work in garden.

Lighting up

There were no street lights in medieval times. People lit their homes with candles or, most often, reeds dipped in fat, called rushlights. The light they gave was very dim.

Rushlights could be put in holders on the wall, or carried in a holder. So you could light your way through the village in the pitch dark of night with a rushlight. But you would still not see very far around you.

The villagers of Cuxham had a steady pattern of life. Was it always calm and peaceful? Did the villagers keep the law, or did they break it? The answer is, as you might expect, a bit of both. Most of the time the villagers tried to get along as best they could with each other. They depended on each other a lot. But they did fall out, lie, steal and cheat, if they thought they could get away with it.

How do we know?

We know what went on from the College records of the manor court. The manor court arranged agreements between the College and villagers. It fined people for not doing their work days, or for doing things that they should not, like grazing their animals on College land. It also told them to pay their debts. The court could fine people, or order them to do extra days of work service.

What don't we know?

We don't know much about serious crimes, like murder, because these were tried by Royal courts in nearby towns. Historians think that fights that ended in violent death were common in medieval times, in towns and villages. The punishment for murder was death, which was also the punishment for serious theft.

Cuxham crimes

Manor court fines:

In 1315 Robert Oldman was taken to court for keeping his animals on College land. He was not fined then, but in 1333 he was taken to the court for the same thing, and this time he was fined 1s for every year he had done this.

In 1320 John Green was fined for letting his sheep graze on the College land.

In 1340 Robert Oldman's son John was fined for stealing some wood from the lord's land the night before Midsummer's Day, probably for the bonfire (see page 51)!

More serious crimes:

In 1290 there was an investigation into the death of a Robert Oldman (possibly the father of the 1315 reeve) because it could have been murder.

In 1374 Ellis Miller of Cuxham was arrested and imprisoned in Wallingford for a serious theft, for which he was sentenced to death. He managed to escape, and was never seen again.

This boy is stealing cherries. He has filled his hood with them. The owner of the tree obviously wants to beat the boy. Many small crimes were dealt with on the spot like this one. But you had to be careful. In 1324 Emma Latter beat a boy whom she caught stealing wood from her house. He died of the beating and she was sentenced to death for murder.

Source A

THE PILLORY

THE STOCKS

What about the rest of the country?

Records from other parts of the country suggest that Cuxham was a typical village. Towns tended to have a higher crime rate. This is hardly surprising. There were more people, and more things to steal. There was more opportunity to steal too, with crowds of people, many of whom did not know each other. There was a law which said that if anyone saw a crime committed, or was attacked they could call out and everyone who was close enough to hear them had to help them or they could be fined. This was called raising the **hue and cry**. It was especially useful in towns and people were fined for not acting on it. The most common crime was stealing. Most people who stole did so because they were poor. They would steal things that could be swapped for food and were worth less than 6d. If you stole goods worth less than 6d it was a minor crime. If the goods were worth more than 6d you could be sentenced to death for the theft.

The problem of punishment

There were no prisons in early medieval times. Important people could be locked up in Royal castles, like the Tower of London. Some towns had small lock-ups, mainly used for keeping people in until they went to court, not for punishment. All that was left was either to take money or land away from the criminal or punish them physically. Minor crimes were punished by putting people in stocks or pillories, so people could throw stones or rotten food or worse at them. People could be left there for a few hours, or even days. Major crimes were punished by death.

Source B

During the medieval period the government set up more courts and employed people to enforce laws. Even so, an Italian visitor in about 1500 said:

It is the easiest thing in the world to get arrested here. You can be arrested at the request of any other person, and there is no punishment for making false accusations. You cannot get released at all unless a jury of twelve men say you are innocent.

Such severe measures should make England safe. Not a bit of it! There are so many thieves in the country that few like to travel alone in the country, except in the middle of the day. Hardly anyone likes to go out at night, especially in London. Despite all the arrests the English are constantly robbing and murdering people in the streets.

Distraint:— Taking goods to pay a fine...

TUG PULL

FINES

Some of the punishments given out for minor crimes.

A crime wave?

Source B says the English were *constantly robbing and murdering people in the streets.* Were they? We have to remember the person who wrote this came from another country. He would probably have been warned of the dangers of a foreign country before he came away. He would also have stood out as a good target for thieves.

At various times during the medieval period, the kings of England tried to take over the neighbouring countries of Wales, Scotland and Ireland. When and why did they do this?

Why did they try to take over?

The reasons the English kings wanted more land were simple – security and expansion.

- **Security:** Wales, Scotland and Ireland were close to England – two of the countries were actually joined to England. As long as they were separate countries they were a threat. Firstly, there was the threat of raids over the borders with England, especially by the Welsh and the Scots. This happened regularly. Secondly, Wales, Scotland and Ireland made wonderful allies for England's enemies. They gave a perfect foothold for an invading army.

- **Expansion:** When England was strong it was natural for its kings to try to take more land. All medieval kings saw it as part of their job to expand their kingdoms. Strong English rulers were often trying to expand their lands in France, as well as into Wales, Scotland and Ireland.

When did they try to take over?

The English kings tried to take over when they were most powerful in England. This was when the English lords supported the King and were not squabbling between themselves.

Which country to attack?

The English kings decided where to attack depending on a number of things:

- How aggressive the people of the other countries were. If the Welsh were minding their own business, but the Scots kept raiding over the border with England, then the king decided he needed to get the Scots under control.
- How strong the rulers of each country were. It is always easier to attack countries with weak rulers than to attack countries with strong rulers.

Source A

This painting shows King John of Scotland, kneeling to swear an oath of **fealty** (obedience) to Edward I in 1296. John is accepting that Scotland belongs to Edward, but that Edward will let John rule it.

Swearing fealty

All through the medieval period, the English kings wanted the Welsh, Scottish and Irish kings to swear fealty. If they did this they were saying that their countries really belonged to the English kings.

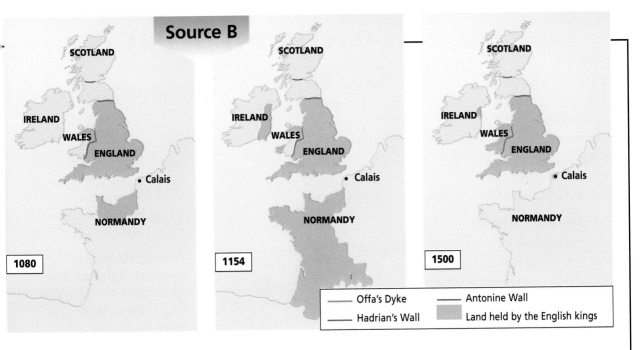

The boundaries of the lands held by English kings in 1080, 1154 and 1500. All through the medieval period, all rulers tried to capture as much land as they could. If they did not take land a neighbouring king might take some of their land instead.

Enemies of the English?

The English saw Ireland, Wales and Scotland as obvious places to conquer. The people in those countries, not surprisingly, saw the borders of England as places from which to raid and steal. The English had been the enemy for a long time.

There were barriers built along England's borders with Wales and Scotland long before 1066. They marked a natural stopping point for conquerors and a natural starting place for further conquest. The Romans built two walls to keep out the Scots – Hadrian's Wall (built in AD 122) and the Antonine Wall (built in AD 241). Offa's Dyke was built between Wales and England in about AD 780, following the line of earlier walls. The sea was Ireland's natural barrier.

Friends of the English?

Welsh, Scots and Irish kings and nobles knew the English wanted a foothold in their lands. When they needed help from English armies – to crush a rebellion, or to start one – they promised to obey the English kings. The English made promises in return. Neither side trusted the other, and they did not always keep their promises.

Turning points

The next three units will look at turning points in the relationship between England and each of these countries. They were not the only turning points, but many historians see them as the most significant.

John Balliol

In 1290, when Margaret, Queen of Scotland died, there were so many people claiming the Scottish throne that the Scots decided to ask Edward I to help them decide who had the best claim. Edward decided on John Balliol, thinking he would be easy to control.

In 1292 Balliol was crowned as King John I. Edward demanded that King John swear fealty for Scotland, as well as his lands in England. John refused, made an alliance with the French and went to war with England. He lost. The English took over. John I died in exile in 1315.

Ireland attracted medieval kings far less than Wales or Scotland. There were reasons which made it harder to control:

- it was separated from England by the sea
- it was harder to get to
- it was a poor country
- it was big and split up into lots of kingdoms.

A reason to invade

The Irish kings often fought among themselves. Early English kings did not get involved in these battles. But in 1166, King Henry II was made a very tempting offer. Dermot McMurrough, King of Leinster [one of the Irish kingdoms], was driven out of Ireland. He fled to England. Dermot said that if Henry helped him regain Leinster he would swear fealty to Henry. Could Henry trust Dermot? Henry was not sure. He said he would not lead an army to Ireland himself, but gave Dermot permission to ask the English lords for help.

Too successful?

Dermot asked some English lords to help. The most important was Richard de Clare, called 'Strongbow'. By 1168, with the help of Strongbow, Dermot had Leinster back. Strongbow and his army of over a thousand men captured the city of Dublin, too. Strongbow married Dermot's daughter, Eva. When Dermot died in 1171, Strongbow took over Leinster. Henry II was worried because Strongbow was getting too powerful. His Irish lands were his own; he had not given Henry an oath of fealty for them. Might he attack England? Strongbow saw Henry was considering a fight. He went back to England and gave his Irish lands to Henry. Then he swore an oath of fealty for them. Henry then went back with Strongbow to Ireland and many other Irish kings also swore fealty to him, fearing the size of Henry and Strongbow's armies together.

Source A

Later English kings saw the early settlement of Ireland as a failure. They wanted a group of people running the country who were on their side. In the Laws of Kilkenny, made in 1336, the kings complained:

While at the time of the conquest of Ireland they spoke their own language, now many of them have given up this and their old way of life. Instead they use the language and the ways of life of the Irish. They have married into and fought with the King's Irish enemies.

Source B

A medieval Irish carving. Irish lords had long hair and beards. The Normans, who had very short hair and no beards, thought this made the Irish look wild and savage.

WHO WAS DERMOT MCMURROUGH?

Dermot McMurrough sparked off the first real English settlement of Ireland. He was a large man, fierce and warlike. He seems to have been quick to pick a fight. In 1131, aged about 20, he had an argument with the Abbess of Kildare. He is said to have settled the argument by taking her away from the Abbey, killing all 140 nuns and burning the Abbey to the ground as he went.

Dermot was always fighting other Irish kings, then becoming their ally, then falling out again. In 1152 he and Turlough O'Connor invaded Breifne. Tiernan O'Rourke, Lord of Breifne, was away at the time. They burned his castles and Dermot took Tiernan's wife, Devorgill, back to Leinster. Some people said she went willingly, because Tiernan was cruel, but by 1153 she had returned to him. It was Tiernan O'Rourke who in 1166, drove Dermot McMurrough out of Leinster, burning his castles and banishing him over the sea.

Dermot recaptured Leinster with English help. Together, he and the English took more land, including the city of Dublin. Other Irish kings tried to stop Dermot. They took one of his sons captive and threatened to kill him if Dermot did not stop. Dermot told them to go ahead, and they did.

Dermot died in 1171, probably of an infected wound.

A Norman knight in Ireland, from about 1200. He has English armour, but has grown long hair and a beard, like the Irish.

One monk wrote of Dermot:
His hand was against everyone, and everyone's hand was against him. He died of an awful unknown disease. He rotted while he was still living. This was a miracle from God and the Irish saints whose churches he burnt. He died without repenting, without making a will and without a priest, just as his evil deeds deserve.

Devorgill outlived Dermot McMurrough and Tiernan O'Rourke (who died in 1172). She died in 1193, aged 85.

Henry II did what the Normans always did in land they had just taken over. He built castles and moved in people he could trust to run things. Many of these people married into Irish families, and took on Irish ways. But some did not. The Irish were hostile to those who did not change. The scene was set for a conflict between the Irish and the English which became a clash of religions too, and which ran into the twentieth century.

No good deeds?

Dermot McMurrough burned and looted the homes of people who angered him – even churches and monasteries. He had churches and abbeys built, too, perhaps to apologise to God.

Wales until 1272

In 1066 Wales was ruled by several Welsh princes. The Norman kings chose strong, loyal lords to run the lands along the Welsh border. They gave these lords the right to call up armies and build castles – powers far greater than other English lords. These lords gradually took over much of south Wales, which was flatter and easier to fight in. But the princes of Gwynedd, in north Wales, were stronger. They never swore fealty to the English kings.

A new king

When Henry III's son, Edward I, became King he made it clear to the English lords that he was in charge. He then set out to make the same thing clear to the Welsh. As always, Gwynedd was the biggest problem, ruled by Llewelyn ap Gryffyd. In 1277, Edward sent soldiers overland, and a fleet of ships to the Welsh coast. The ships cut Gwynedd off from the island of Anglesey, which grew most of their food. The Welsh were forced to hide out in the mountains of Snowdonia. They could not stay there forever. Llewelyn had to surrender and swear fealty. In 1282 Llewelyn's brother, David, rebelled against Edward. Llewelyn joined him. By 1283 the rebellion had been brutally put down and Llewelyn and David were dead.

The final conquest?

By 1301, Edward felt he had the Welsh under control. He gave his son the title 'Prince of Wales', which he said was a gesture of peace. In a way it was. Wales was the only part of England allowed to have its own prince. But Edward was also underlining the conquest of Wales. Llewelyn had been Prince of Wales. Now the Prince of Wales would also be King of England. Wales never again had its own ruler.

Source A

The Chronicle of Lanercost, written at the time, describes the punishment given to David ap Gryffyd:

David had his entrails cut out of his stomach, for being a traitor. He was then hung, for being a thief. His arms and legs were cut off, for being a rebel. They were then sent to four parts of England, as a warning and a celebration. The right arm was sent to York, the left arm to Bristol. The right leg went to Northampton and the left to Hereford. His head was bound with iron to stop it falling apart as it rotted. It was sent to London and put on show on the walls.

Source B

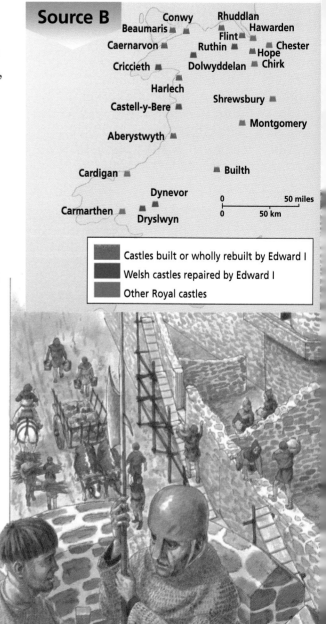

Conwy • Rhuddlan • Beaumaris • Hawarden • Flint • Caernarvon • Ruthin • Chester • Hope • Criccieth • Dolwyddelan • Chirk • Harlech • Shrewsbury • Castell-y-Bere • Montgomery • Aberystwyth • Cardigan • Builth • Dynevor • Carmarthen • Dryslwyn

0 — 50 miles
0 — 50 km

■ Castles built or wholly rebuilt by Edward I
■ Welsh castles repaired by Edward I
■ Other Royal castles

Just one example: Conwy Castle

Castle builders

Edward I's Master Builder, James St. George, started work on Conwy in 1283, with a team of experienced builders. He used the most up-to-date castle design in the defences of the castle, and in the arrangements for daily life. (Lavatories were built out over a stream to carry away the waste.) The men who did the day-to-day work came from all over the country. They worked from the beginning of February to the end of October, from sunrise to sunset, six days a week.

Building costs

Conwy cost £20,000 to build. That would come to well over £2 million now – and that was for just one castle. It was finished enough to live in by the autumn of 1287, although building work carried on into 1292. Conwy was big, but was so well designed that it only needed 30 men to defend and maintain it: 15 crossbow men, 1 chaplain, 1 blacksmith, 1 builder, 1 carpenter and 11 others, mostly watchmen.

Making a point?

The Welsh prince Llewelyn the Great (father of the Llewelyn Edward executed in 1283) was buried at Conwy Abbey. Edward I had the Abbey moved, stone by stone, to a different place. He knocked down the town of Conwy. He built a new town and castle there. Conwy was one of Edward I's first new castles in Wales.

Edward chose to build a castle at Conwy because it was a good defensive site, but he chose it for another reason too. Conwy had been the most important town in Wales, the nearest thing to a Welsh capital. He was making the point that the English were in charge and were there to stay.

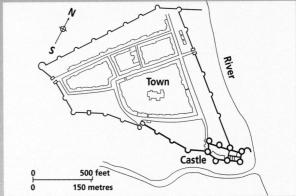

Source C

A plan of Conwy Castle and the town, and a modern artist's drawing of the castle when it was nearly finished.

Stone walls

Castles were big. It took a lot of stone slabs to build a castle. Stone was heavy, and difficult to transport on mud roads. So castle builders used local stone wherever possible. There are old stone quarries near many castles.

This is why castles in different parts of the country are different colours. Conwy and Goodrich, for example, are a reddish colour. Rochester is greyish white. It depends on the colour of the local stone.

The Normans soon found a foothold in Scotland. David I, who became King of Scotland in 1124, was also Earl of Huntingdon in England. He had to swear fealty for these lands. He needed Norman help to control the Scottish lords. He gave land to the Normans who helped him. So the kings of Scotland and England were friendly. Would they join forces?

Normans or Scots?

England and Scotland could only join forces if David swore fealty, giving his Scottish lands away. He had no intention of doing this. The important families in Scotland were now Norman, but they had sworn an oath of fealty to David for their lands. They owed the King of England nothing, despite having families in England. They married into Scottish families, and saw themselves as Scots.

Independent or part of a kingdom?

The English and the Scots argued over whether Scotland was a free country or whether it was held by an oath of fealty to the English kings. Because the Scottish kings still swore fealty for their English lands, things were confused. Weak English kings accepted Scotland's independence. Strong kings invaded and forced the Scottish kings to swear fealty. The situation erupted under Edward I.

The Hammer of the Scots

In 1296, Edward invaded Scotland and forced the Scottish King John to swear fealty. He returned to England, leaving the Earl of Surrey as Governor of Scotland. He forced the Scots to pay taxes and fight in the English army. The Scots, led by William Wallace, rebelled and drove the English out. Edward marched back to Scotland. This time it took longer to take over. But by 1305 he had defeated the rebels and executed Wallace. He was nick-named 'Hammer of the Scots'.

A final answer?

Led by Robert Bruce, the Scots rose against the English again in 1306. But Edward's army fought back and Bruce was forced into hiding. Then, in 1307, Edward I died. His son, Edward II, was less keen to fight. Bruce recaptured the Scottish castles. Edward marched to Scotland. But it was too late – Bruce was too strong. The English were defeated at Bannockburn in 1314. Edward II never recaptured Scotland. In 1327 he died and his son, Edward III, agreed that Scotland was a free and independent nation.

One nation

It was not until the thirteenth century that the Scots began to see themselves as one nation. Edward I made them more united by forcing their King to swear fealty, seizing the Stone of Scone (the seat on which all Scottish kings were crowned) and the Scottish Crown Jewels, too.

Source A

When Alexander III came to swear fealty to Edward I for his English land he was pressed to do the same for Scotland. He replied:

No one has the right to ask me to swear fealty for my kingdom of Scotland, except God. To God alone will I do this.

Source B

King David II of Scotland with King Edward III of England. They are shaking hands as equals. Compare this to Source A on page 54.

ROBERT BRUCE A ROYAL REBEL

Robert Bruce's grandfather claimed the Scottish throne in 1290. John Balliol was the other claimant. Both the Bruces and the Balliols were descended from the Scottish king David I. The Scots asked Edward I to decide who should be king. He chose Balliol. So the Bruce family had a grudge against Edward I. Despite this, when Edward defeated William Wallace's rebels at Falkirk in 1298, Robert Bruce and his father swore fealty to Edward.

A losing battle?

In March 1306 Bruce was crowned King of Scotland at Scone. Edward I set off with an army immediately. Bruce had to go into hiding. Edward could not catch and punish Bruce, so he punished his family instead. About twenty male relatives were executed. His wife, Elizabeth, and his 12 year old daughter, Marjorie, were put in prison. One sister, Christina, was put in a nunnery. His other sister, Mary, and the Countess of Buchan (who crowned him King) were shut in cages and hung from the walls of Berwick and Roxburgh castles. And all the while Bruce was in hiding, with a few loyal people, trying to survive in one of the worst winters in living memory.

Never give in

At this point, many people would have given in. Bruce did not. Some people say he was encouraged by seeing a spider patiently re-spinning the threads of its web. Whether or not it was true, the story was widely told to show Bruce's determination, which paid off. Bruce set up constant raids on the English and the castles they held. His people cut off supplies, burned crops and attacked the Scots who supported the English. In 1307, Edward I died. His son, Edward II, disbanded the army raised to march on Scotland. Now Bruce could gather strength.

Victory at last

Slowly, Bruce began to win. By the summer of 1313 only Stirling Castle held out. Edward II had to march against Bruce. Edward had a huge army, about 17,000 men. Bruce had about 6,000. They met at Bannockburn in Scotland. The English were beaten. They refused to accept the Scots were a separate nation. So Bruce took the war to England, raiding lands on the borders and forcing English lords to swear fealty to him. The Scots were determined to force the English to accept Scottish independence. They wrote in the Declaration of Arbroath: *as long as a hundred of us remain alive, we will not bow to English rule. It is not for glory, riches or honour that we fight: it is for liberty alone.* In 1327 Edward III accepted Scottish independence. Robert Bruce died in 1329.

Source C

Robert Bruce, painted in 1306.

Bannockburn

The English had a much bigger army than the Scots at Bannockburn, almost three times bigger. They also had far more horsemen. Yet they lost. Why? The weather had been wet. So the horses found it hard to get a grip on the steep slippery ground near the burn (stream).

An Englishman who was there later said: *Many nobles and others slid into the river with their horses in the crush. Many could not get themselves out again.* The English army panicked and fled.

In medieval times, most people lived in villages. However, between 1100 and 1300 towns grew in size and many new ones sprung up. Why was this? There were many reasons. More and more villeins were becoming freemen. Villeins bought their freedom and many moved away from their villages to live and work in the towns. Some simply ran away, believing that life in a town could be no worse than their lives in the countryside.

Towns and trade

Between 1100 and 1300, people working in the countryside produced more and more food. This they sold in local markets in nearby towns. More people came to the towns to trade, and this encouraged the townspeople to provide the sorts of services traders wanted: they brewed ale, baked bread and made clothes. People with special skills like dyeing and weaving came to live in towns where cloth was made. And so towns grew and flourished.

What were towns like?

Most medieval towns were a jumble of houses, shops, market stalls, animals and people, all jammed in together along narrow, sometimes cobbled, streets. There were often no drains to take away rainwater and waste from buildings. Clean water was difficult to get hold of. Towns were very smelly places!

London: big problems

London was the biggest town in England. In 1066 about 10,000 people lived there. That is about the same number of people as a quarter of the crowd watching a Liverpool match at Anfield. One hundred years later, the population of London was around 25,000. Problems which London had with sewage, street cleaning and clean water would probably be the same, or worse, than those of other towns.

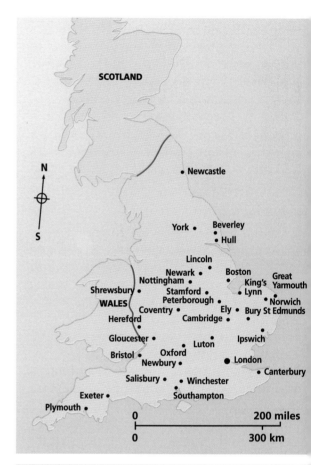

The main towns in England in the 15th century.

Polluted water

Until about 1200, Londoners got their water from springs and wells. However, this water slowly became more and more polluted (dirty) until it wasn't really fit to drink. Where did this pollution come from? Brewers, dyers and tanners set up their workshops near the river Thames. They threw all kinds of rubbish into the river. People also tipped human waste into the river. All this muck eventually seeped back into the wells and springs.

From about 1237 Londoners began to build systems of pipes from hollowed out tree trunks or lead to bring fresh water from the countryside. Water sellers collected this water from huge stone sinks and sold it. Most people preferred to drink beer. It was safer.

Source A

This drawing of London Bridge was made in about 1500. You can see how crowded together the houses were. There were public toilets on the Bridge, and these emptied straight into the river.

Source B

Part of a letter written in 1349 from Edward III to the Lord Mayor of London.

The human waste and other filth lying in the streets and lanes in the city and suburbs must be removed with all speed. The King has learned how the city and suburbs are so foul with the filth from out of the houses that the air is infected and the city poisoned to the danger of men.

Filthy streets

The streets of London were often filthy. People threw absolutely everything they didn't need into the streets: rotting fruit and vegetables, old leather bottles, the innards of slaughtered animals, along with human and animal waste.

Everyone had problems with human waste. Some toilets emptied into rivers and streams, which all ran into the river Thames. Others emptied into cess-pits, which had to be specially emptied. The workmen who did this were called 'gongfermers', and were paid well.

Dirty houses

Inside many houses it wasn't much better. The houses of the poorer people were made out of wattle and daub (sticks, mud, muck and horse-hair), with straw thatched roofs and rushes on the floor. Unless the house owners were careful, rats lived in the thatch, lice, bed bugs and fleas in the walls and all kinds of nasty things in the beer. Grease, gnawed bones and dirty rags could be found under the rushes on the floor. This does not mean that people did not try to keep their houses clean. Most people did. But in towns this was often a losing battle.

Source C

This is the conclusion of a jury in the City of London when, in 1321, they investigated complaints about a right of way being blocked.

The jury decided that the lane called Ebbegate (which runs between the tenements of Master John de Pulteneye and Master Thomas at Wytte) used to be a right of way for all men until it was closed up by Thomas at Wytte and William Hockle who got together and built toilets which stuck out from the walls of the houses. From these toilets human filth falls onto the heads of the passersby.

Dirt and disease

People in medieval times did not have the technology to find out about germs. They did not know that germs existed, nor how they bred. They tried to explain the causes of disease from the knowledge they had. Some of the things they thought caused disease were the planets, bad air and God. They did see dirt as being linked to disease, but only by its effect on the air, as Source B shows.

Town charters

Many towns grew and became prosperous between 1100 and 1300. Townspeople began to want their independence from the local lord. They wanted to choose their own officials to run the town. They wanted to make their own rules about, for example, markets and fairs and what time the town gates should be closed. They wanted to hold law courts and collect their own taxes. Various kings granted charters to towns giving them these sorts of powers. In return, the town paid certain taxes to the king every year. King Richard I and King John granted more charters to towns than any other monarchs. This was partly because they needed money for their wars.

Lincoln's charter

Lincoln was granted its charter in 1129. This meant that the townspeople could choose who ran their town. At the beginning of the 1200s Lincoln had a **mayor** and ten other officials to run the city. As the city of Lincoln grew, more and more people were needed to run it. By the end of the 1400s, a large slice of the city's income was being paid out to city officials, and people were complaining that the officials were costing far too much.

Wool and woollen cloth

English wool was the best in Europe, and some of the best English wool came from the sheep around Lincoln. In the 1100s and 1200s English wool was sold to other countries. When something is sold to another country we call it an **export**. Wool was England's largest export and the main source of England's wealth. Most of the wool produced in England went to the weavers in Flanders. They wove beautifully fine woollen cloth and sold it to rich people all over Europe, including England. English weavers at that time wove thicker, rougher cloth. These materials were used for clothing the army and for making strong clothes for working people. It wasn't until the 1300s that English weavers began to make fine cloth themselves.

Source A

From the medieval town laws of Lincoln.

If any married woman follow a craft within the city, which her husband has nothing to do with, she shall be counted as an unmarried woman in connection with anything to do with her craft. And if a complaint is made against her, she shall answer it as an unmarried woman. And if she is condemned, she shall be sent to prison until she, and the person making the complaint, can come to an agreement.

Source B

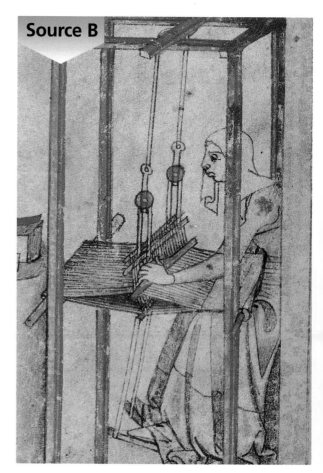

This picture of a woman weaving cloth was drawn sometime between 1350 and 1375.

Lincoln grows

Lincoln was joined to the port of Boston and to other towns by a network of waterways. Wool and cloth could be moved around easily without having to depend upon packhorses using roads that were often too muddy to travel on. Lincoln was such a great cloth centre that foreigners, usually from Flanders, were allowed to trade there and to operate out of the port of Boston. In 1326 Lincoln became a staple town – one of the few towns through which wool and woollen cloth could be imported and exported.

Guilds

Craftsmen were skilled workers. They were butchers and fishmongers, stonemasons, shoemakers and goldsmiths – and clothworkers. Each craft had its own **guild**. The guild made rules about wages, prices and ways of working in each craft. Young people – usually young men – who wanted to learn a trade got their families to pay for them to be **apprenticed** to a master in the trade they wanted to learn. They lived with the master's family for a set number of years while they learned about their chosen trade. After this an apprentice could become a **journeyman** and work for himself. When he was really good he became a **master.**

Lincoln had eleven different trade guilds. They all had their own rules – and some of them had yearly feasts and all sorts of different festivals.

Source C

Market prices and tolls fixed by the city of Lincoln in 1361. There were eleven markets in Lincoln. They dealt in such things as meat, fish, corn, poultry, animal skins, malt and cloth.

10 eggs	**1d**
3 roast thrushes	**2d**
Roast pig	**8d**
Roast chicken in pasty	**8d**
On every horse bought or sold	**1d**
On every ox bought or sold	**1/2d**
On 24 sheep	**1d**
On a quarter (291 litres) of corn	**1d**
On each cart	**2d**

Joining a guild

To join a guild you had to have worked as an apprentice and a journeyman. You had to show the guild members that you could do good quality work. Some guilds asked you to make something specially, as a test. Others just looked at the work you were doing in your job.

Most important of all, you had to pay to join a guild. No matter how good your work was, you could not join if you could not afford the fee.

Source D

This painting, made in 1482, shows a guild master judging the work of men who want to become masters. He will decide whether or not they are good enough.

What was a merchant?

Merchants bought goods from people who made or grew them and then sold the goods to other people at a higher price. They were middlemen, and some became very rich. Of course, merchants took risks. They had to have the money to buy goods before they sold them on. They could not be really certain of selling them at a higher price. Even so, some merchants became very rich, richer than many of the most important families in the country. In medieval times it was easier to move goods by water than by roads, so many merchants lived in or near a port.

Abingdon	Soap Clay Iron	Reading	Tin
Alton	Wine Dye Clay Resin Salt	Romsey	Wine Fish Garlic Silk Coal Iron Dye
Andover	Onions Soap Wax Iron Fish		
Bristol	Dye Soap Wine	Salisbury	Wine Fish Dye Flax Soap Canvas Dried fruits Timber Building materials Household furnishings
Exeter	Dye		
Gloucester	Dye Soap Oil		
Honiton	Dye	Wilton	Dye Oil Wine Flax
Leicester	Dye	Winchester	Fish Wine Oil Salt Garlic Iron Soap Dye
Oxford	Wine Dye Millstones		

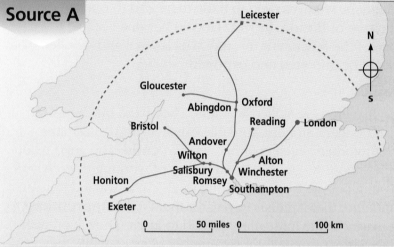

Source A

This map shows the goods that were brought into Southampton, and where they came from.

Source B

A Southampton merchant

Walter Fetplace was a merchant working from Southampton in the 1400s. He bought cloth dyes from Italian merchants, and sold them to dyers working in Salisbury and Winchester– towns a few miles from Southampton. Walter, like most merchants, also dealt in other goods. He bought and sold salt, fish, fruit and wine as well as the dyes.

Trade routes in England

By about 1350 there were hundreds of roads linking trading towns and cities. Strings of packhorses plodded along them with their heavy loads. Source A shows the cartways used by merchants and packhorses heading for Southampton. Some of the goods would be sold in Southampton itself. They would be sold in shops or from market stalls like those in Source B

A medieval street with shops and market stalls, painted in 1460.

DAME CLARAMUNDA – A MEDIEVAL BUSINESSWOMAN

Dame Claramunda was a rich and successful Southampton merchant. She was so good at her job that in 1258 she won the contract to supply King Henry III with wine from France. How had she got to this position? She had been married twice, and both her husbands had died. In Southampton and elsewhere widows could carry on their husband's business.

Dame Claramunda combined two successful businesses and made them even better. She lived in a large house on the harbour, where she could keep an eye on port activities, and owned other houses and shops in the town. When she died – she had no children – she left a lot of silver and jewellery to churches and monasteries in and around Southampton. Rich people often did this. Perhaps they thought it would speed them into heaven.

Trade routes to Europe

Southampton, as you can see from the maps, is a port. In medieval times it was very well positioned for trading with all the important ports in Europe. Southampton got its Charter in 1199 by which time it was an important port.

Source C

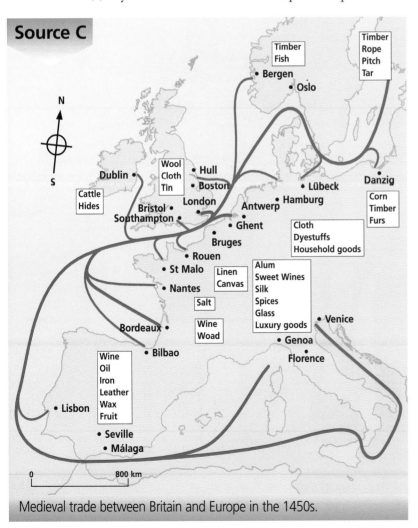

Medieval trade between Britain and Europe in the 1450s.

Thomas Betson

Thomas Betson was an English wool merchant. He bought wool from the English 'wool growers', as sheep farmers were called. He packed the wool, following strict government rules. He then sent it to Calais. It was sent from London, Southampton or other ports, depending where he bought it.

Before it was allowed to leave the country, Customs Officials checked that the wool was properly packed and weighed. It was then sealed up with a Customs seal and a guild seal.

Betson travelled to Europe to sell the wool. He sold it wherever he could get the best price. This was usually in the Netherlands. He spent a lot of time abroad, visiting wool markets and fairs.

Bells not clocks

People got up at daybreak. The bell-ringer rang the town bell and the town gates were opened. The work of the day could begin.

At night the bell-ringer rang the **curfew** bell. The town gates were closed and everyone had to be inside their own houses.

Baths and lavatories

People went to public bath-houses. They had to pay to use them. People either used outside lavatories, or, when there were inside ones, they emptied through a hole in the wall into a cesspit or onto the street.

Having a baby

Having a baby was a dangerous business. Many mothers and babies died. This was partly because of infection and partly because there was very little that anyone could do to hurry up a difficult labour. Babies died for many reasons, but mainly because they were stressed by a long labour, starved of oxygen or were being born feet or bottom, instead of head, first. Mothers died because of infection or because they bled to death. Most women had friends or a midwife to help them while they were having a baby.

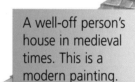

A well-off person's house in medieval times. This is a modern painting.

Getting ill

Doctors charged high fees. Most townspeople went to the local **apothecary** if someone in their family was ill. He would sell them herbs, drugs or magic spells which might make the person better. Sometimes they worked; sometimes the person would have got better anyway; sometimes the person died. No one knew whether they would have died anyway, or whether the apothecary's cure killed them off.

Source A

Cooking

Not every house had a kitchen. Women or servants took the ingredients to a specialised cook, like a baker or pie maker. They would make, for example, pastries crammed full of fruit, or chopped ham, soft cheese, larks or eels. Herbs and spices were used to flavour food, especially if it was beginning to go off.

Cooks used thyme and mustard seed, rosemary and garlic. Crusaders brought spices like pepper and cloves back from the East.

Possessions

The house in the picture belonged to a well-off craftsman. But if you look in all the rooms of the house you will see that medieval people had fewer possessions than people do now.

They had less furniture. They did not have carpets or curtains. They had just enough pots and pans to cook with. They had fewer clothes – maybe a change of clothes and several changes of underwear.

Everything that people owned was made from natural materials – wooden furniture, wool or linen clothes and leather shoes.

Kitchens

Kitchens were often built in the yard. This was because no one wanted a fire spreading from the kitchen to the main house. Most kitchens had pestles and mortars for grinding up herbs and spices; bunches of twigs for whisking eggs, cream and batters; long handled pots and pans and scouring sand for washing up.

A devastating plague struck East and West. Whole populations vanished. The entire world changed. An Arab historian who lived through the Black Death wrote this.

What was the plague?

The plague, also called the Black Death, was two related illnesses (see **Plague facts**). It swept across much of the known world in 1346 – 53. It killed animals, birds and millions of people.

Where did it start?

The Black Death first struck in Asia, in 1346. It spread rapidly across Europe following the sea and land routes used by traders and travellers. Once it began to move it spread at an alarming pace.

How did it spread?

People at the time saw that the plague was spread by travellers and traders. But they were not sure how. They were sure that just one person could infect a town. Many towns, ports and cities tried to shut travellers out and sent ships away. The plague moved quickly through towns because people were crowded together and there were more rats and other animals to pass on the disease.

Plague facts

There were two sorts of plague:

Bubonic plague was carried by rat fleas, but could pass on to animal and human fleas. People and animals were infected by being bitten by the fleas.
Symptoms:
- cold, tingling feeling, tiredness
- swellings (called buboes), mainly in the groin or armpit
- swellings go black, blisters or black blotches appear all over.

The illness lasted 5-10 days. People could recover, although most died. Plague fleas die in winter, and this usually stopped plague outbreaks. But the plague did not stop in the winters of 1346–9. Perhaps this was because these winters were mild, so fleas survived. Also, bubonic plague could change into pneumonic plague.

Pneumonic plague could be passed from person to person, in their saliva. So being coughed on by an infected victim could be enough to pass the disease on.
Symptoms:
- chest pains
- difficulty breathing
- coughing up blood and pus.

The illness was fast-working. People nearly always died within two or three days.

Source A

Burying early plague victims in Tournai, in the Netherlands.

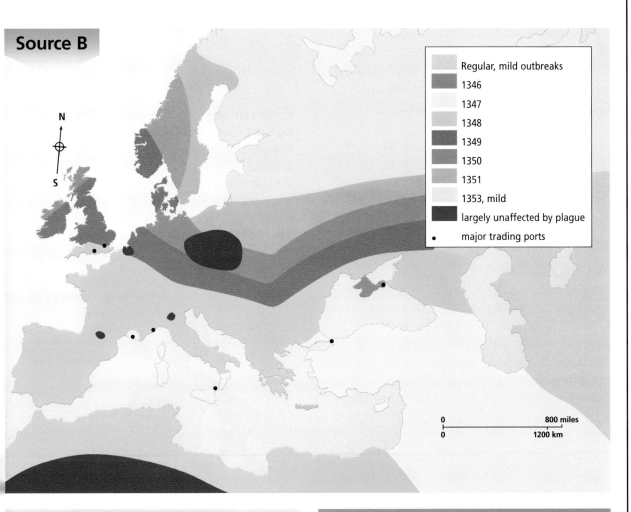

Source B

Regular, mild outbreaks
1346
1347
1348
1349
1350
1351
1353, mild
largely unaffected by plague
• major trading ports

0   800 miles
0   1200 km

How the plague spread, 1346–1353.

Source C

A historian in the Italian city of Padua at the time of the plague said it was a punishment from God.

God struck a warning blow first, in the East. He struck Tartars, Turks and other unbelievers [non-Christians] with the plague. Then he sent a great earthquake to terrify Christians everywhere.

After this the plague, which was more devastating than anything ever before, crossed the sea and came to Italy, Germany and France. It spread through almost the whole world. This terrible sickness was carried by infected people from the East who, by sight, or touch, or breathing on others, killed everyone.

No time to care?

At first, plague victims were buried in wooden coffins in hastily dug graves. Later, things got worse. An Italian describing the plague in Florence said the bodies were piled up in a mass grave and covered in soil: *then others went on top and another layer of soil. It was like making lasagne with layers of pasta and sauce.*

Why were they spared?

The areas coloured dark purple on the map were places that were hardly touched by the plague. We do not know why this was. It is most likely that they were not on trade routes or they kept strangers away. At the time, many would have thought their prayers saved them.

The best medicine for the plague is to get ready to die and confess your sins. This is better than any cures doctors may suggest. For God sends the plague, and only he can stop it, advised an Italian priest (who was also a doctor) in 1347. Many people believed that God had sent the plague, and it was useless to try to cure it. But there were other ideas about the cause of the plague and how to cure it. What were they?

Did doctors know what to do?

Doctors did not know for sure what caused the plague, nor what would cure it. Some of them admitted they had no idea what to do and left the cities. Some of them used treatments that seemed to work for other diseases, like taking blood from the patient, or giving them herbs as medicine. Some of them tried putting softened bread mixed with herbs on the swellings, to try to draw the infection out. This worked on the wounds, but not on the plague itself, which was already in the patient's bloodstream. Others charged huge sums of money for 'cures' that did not work.

Who else tried to control the plague?

Did anyone else know what caused the plague and what to do about it? The people who ran some of the cities tried to make rules to control the plague. They tried to keep the sick people separate and bury the bodies quickly. The cartoon on page 73 shows you some of the ideas that people had about the plague.

Dying properly

Catholics believed that to get to Heaven you had to confess your sins to a priest before you died and have a proper burial. Plague victims were often denied both these things. Their families had to watch them die horribly; believing they would never reach Heaven.

Source A

A historian in Padua during the plague described reactions to the plague there.

It was carried by infected people who, by sight, or touch, or breathing on others, killed everyone. It was incurable. It could not be avoided. Wives fled their husbands, fathers their sons, brothers fled each other. Even the house or clothes of a victim could kill. One death in a house was followed by the death of all the rest, right down to the dogs. Doctors admitted that they had no cure for it, indeed, the best of them died of it.

Source B

This doctor is 'bleeding' a patient. He is taking some blood from his body. Doctors believed that the body could produce too much blood. A person who had too much blood in their body became ill.

What worked?

Some of the cures that people tried for the plague worked, even if they were tried for the wrong reasons. Shutting people up stopped them from infecting others. Clearing rubbish from the streets helped too. This was not because it stopped bad air, as people thought, but because there were fewer places for the rats to live and there was less for them to eat.

In January 1349 there were about 110 people over the age of 14 living in Cuxham. Plague struck the village in the winter and spring of 1349. By the end of the year all twelve people who held the villein rights were dead. We do not know about their families. Only four of the eight cottagers survived to March 1352, when the records show that only nine of the villein holdings and two of the cottager holdings were lived in. The first count of the villagers after 1349 was in 1377. There were only 38 people over the age of 14.

Changing people

Simply in terms of numbers the village had suffered a heavy loss. But the loss went deeper than that. For a long time the same families had lived in Cuxham. People from other villages did move in from time to time, but not often. All that changed. Cuxham lost its reeve as well as most of the old tenants. In the years that followed the College had a great deal of trouble finding someone to run the village. They appointed bailiffs who were not villagers, and who only stayed a short time. The villagers came and went again quickly too.

Changing rents

The new villagers took on villein land for rent, not work. The new arrangement was 1 day hoeing, 1 day haymaking, 2 days harvest work and a payment of about 10s. They might do extra work, if so they expected to be paid wages. Many stayed a short time then moved on, to get a better deal somewhere else. Cottagers (who had done less work before the plague) pushed for better rents. Their situation did not change as much. Before 1349 the College expected an income of £40 a year from Cuxham. After 1349 they expected under £11 per year.

Changing crops

The Black Death had a big effect on the crops villagers grew. All over the country there were fewer people to feed. So the villagers grew more fodder crops (animal food). People had started to keep more animals, so fodder made more money than food for humans to eat.

The villagers may well have tried to control the plague by burning the clothes of the victims. But touching the clothes meant they risked infection.

Source A

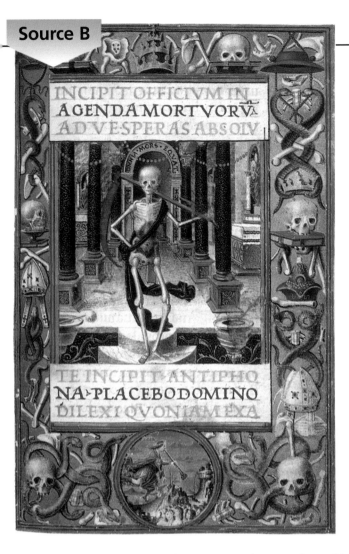

INCIPIT OFFICIVM IN
AGENDA MORTVORV
AD VESPERAS ABSOLV

TE INCIPIT ANTIPHO
NA PLACEBO DOMINO
DILEXI QVONIAM EXA

After 1349, pictures like this one, showing Death as king of all, appeared all over Europe. Living through the plague years made people much more aware of death.

Gone away?

The Cuxham records only tell us what happened to the person who held the land from the College. It does not tell us about their families. Some family members may have lived, but moved to a new place.

WHAT HAPPENED TO PEOPLE IN CUXHAM?

JOHN GREEN
John Green survived the Black Death, as did his son, young John Green. John's son Thomas was not so lucky. He was bailiff from April to June 1349, when he died of the plague. Both John Greens carried on building up the family land. They mainly kept sheep after the Black Death. They took on some extra crop-growing land in Cuxham, but soon gave it up, perhaps because of the problems of finding anyone to do the work.

ROBERT OLDMAN
The Oldman family were devastated by the plague. Robert died in March 1349, while working on the accounts. The College records say: *he died before he could say anything about the fodder for the oxen.* His son John took over. In early April Robert's wife died. John was dead by mid April. We do not know what happened to the other two sons, Richard and Robert, but they are not mentioned in the College records after 1349.

JOAN OVERCHURCH
Joan was an old lady in 1315, so she was dead before the plague struck. Her son, Elias, and his family all died.

HENRY GARDENER
Henry Gardener (who took on a cottager holding with his wife Margery in 1341) survived. He took advantage of the situation. He left his cottager holding and became a villein.

9.4 HOW DID THE BLACK DEATH AFFECT OTHER PLACES?

We have seen how Cuxham was devastated by the plague. But was the plague worse in Cuxham than in other places that it hit?

Source A

Gabriel de Mussis, a monk, wrote of the plague in Italy in 1349:

Scarcely one in seven of the people of Genoa survived. In Venice 70% of the people died. All over Italy people say their areas were the worst hit. It is extraordinarily difficult for me to give an accurate count.

Source B

In 1359, the monk Jean de Vedette wrote about the effects of the plague on France:

In many places not two men lived out of twenty. People died all through 1348 and 1349. Then it stopped. But by then many villages and towns were almost empty. After the plague, people became more mean and greedy than before, even though many were far better off. There was plenty of everything, but people charged more for equipment and food. Wages went up a lot. Only houses were cheap. There were not enough people to rent them. Many have become ruins.

Source C

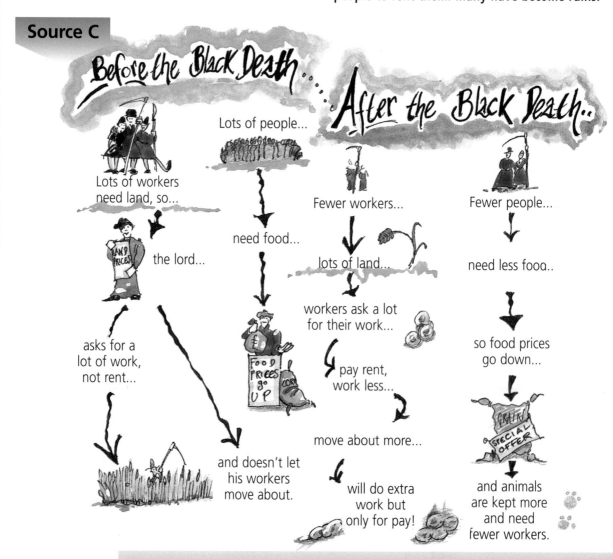

Before the Black Death...

Lots of people...

Lots of workers need land, so...

the lord...

need food...

asks for a lot of work, not rent...

Food prices go up...

and doesn't let his workers move about.

After the Black Death...

Fewer workers...

Fewer people...

lots of land...

need less food...

workers ask a lot for their work...

so food prices go down...

pay rent, work less...

move about more...

will do extra work but only for pay!

and animals are kept more and need fewer workers.

Some effects of the Black Death. Historians think that at least some of these things (like moving from work to money payments of rent) were beginning to happen anyway. The Black Death speeded up the process.

Source D

Source E

A Royal proclomation made in June, 1349, shows another effect of the plague:

Because so many people died in the plague, there are labourers who, seeing there are fewer workers and much work to do, refuse to work unless they are paid huge wages. This is a problem, especially in farming. So any man or woman, free or unfree, who is fit and under the age of sixty must accept any work offered to them.

They should work for the same agreements as in 1346. If they refuse, they will be imprisoned until they agree. Lords do not have to keep agreements they have made this past year, if they are unreasonable. Lords cannot offer such agreements to persuade people to work for them.

Many monasteries cared for the sick as part of their duties. The death rates in places that cared for plague victims was very high. But some places turned plague victims away, just as some parish priests refused to visit people who had the plague.

Source F

Geoffrey Baker, a clerk in Oxfordshire, wrote in the 1340s about the plague:

The whole of England was so badly hit that hardly one person in ten survived. When the churchyards were full, whole fields were used to bury the dead. Courts did not hear cases so justice was disrupted. A few nobles died and countless numbers of ordinary people.

The plague raged for a year and completely emptied many small villages. Hardly anyone dared to have anything to do with the sick.

What can they pay?

After the Black Death, many places carried out surveys of the taxes that villages were supposed to pay and how much they could pay.

These examples from East Yorkshire show that, even in the same area of the country, some places were hit much harder by the Black Death than others.

Village	Tax to pay	Amount paid
South Burton	£7 10s	£5 17s 6d
Willerby	£3	£3
Bubworth	£2 10s	£2
North Ferilby	£2 16s 8d	£0 13s 4d
Skidby	£6 10s	£4

Why did the peasants revolt?

In 1381 there was a serious rebellion in England. This time it wasn't powerful barons rebelling against a weak king or trying to reduce the power of a strong one. This time it was the peasants, led by local gentlemen, who were so angry that they burned, destroyed and killed until they got what they wanted. Or so they thought. What had happened to make them do this?

The Black Death

You have just read about the effects of the Black Death in Europe. Remember that in Cuxham only three people were left to work the land. This happened all over England. Once the people had recovered from the shock and horror of the terrible plague, they began to think about their situation.

Wages

There were far fewer labourers to do all the work on the manors of England. So the ones that were left began to ask for higher wages and fewer hours of work. Some of them asked for their freedom. They often got what they asked for: the lords of the manors were desperate to get their land farmed and their animals looked after. Then, in 1351, King Edward III summoned parliament to make a new law. The law was called the Statute of Labourers and it tried to make sure that the landowners had as many labourers as they wanted – and that they paid them no more than before the Black Death. This made many peasants very angry.

Land

A lot of land was now going to waste. People who, before the Black Death, would never have dreamed of owning land, now could. Often this was not strictly legal, but the wealthier peasants didn't really care. They wanted land, and they were going to get it. They were determined to improve their lot.

John Ball

Some people began to write about how badly society was run. Many of them just wanted the same system, but fairly organised. Others went further. John Ball, a priest in York, preached that all people were created equal by God. He said that Adam and Eve were the first people made by God, and that they were equal.

It was man, and not God, who had made some people lords and others poor peasants. This was dangerous stuff, and really frightened those in power. The peasants were restless enough, and to tell them that they were equal to their masters would only make a bad situation worse. The bishops ordered John Ball not to preach in any church in the diocese of York. He became a travelling priest in the south of England, preaching in the open wherever people would listen to him. He was arrested and imprisoned in Maidstone.

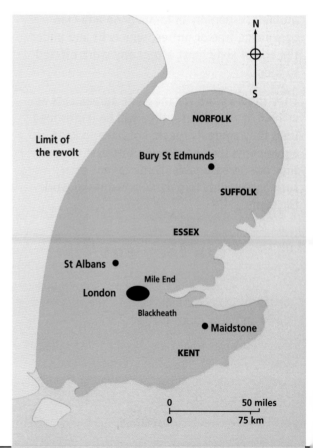

The main centres of revolt in 1381.

Source A

Written in 1370 by a priest called William Langland. This comes from a long story called *Piers Plowman*.

The labourers that have no land and work with their hands will no longer eat the stale vegetables of yesterday. Penny ale will not suit them, nor bacon. They want fresh meat or fish, fried or baked. Unless he is highly paid he will regret the time he was made a workman. Then he curses the King and all the King's justices for making such laws that grieve [are hard on] the labourer.

Source B

This picture of John Ball leading a group of peasants was painted in 1460. They are carrying the royal standard and the cross of St. George to show their loyalty to King Richard II.

Poll tax

The peasants were used to paying rents and taxes to the lord of their manor and to the Church. They were not used to paying taxes to the king. If the king needed money he usually raised it from rich landowners and merchants, not from the peasants. But the war in France was going badly and the king desperately needed more money. So in 1377, parliament introduced a new tax – the Poll Tax. Everybody over the age of fifteen had to pay it, no matter whether they were rich or poor. In 1377 everyone paid 4d and, again in 1379 another 4d. Then, in 1381 everyone was asked to pay 12d. This was the final straw. In Essex, peasants rioted, killed three of the local tax collectors' assistants, stuck their heads on poles and marched around with them. The peasants sent messages to other peasants in Suffolk, Norfolk and Kent, asking them to join the rebellion. Kent peasants, led by Wat Tyler, captured Rochester Castle. They marched on to Maidstone and forced the town gaoler to release John Ball from prison then marched toward London.

The Peasants' Revolt had begun.

Source C

From the Statute of Labourers 1351. This was a law that was intended to make sure landowners had enough labourers and had to pay them as little as possible.

Villeins who are idle and not willing to work without very high wages shall be ordered to work, in the place where they ought to work, receiving the usual wages. Villeins who refuse should be punished and put in prison.

Why just the south?

If you look at the map on page 140, you will see that the Peasants' Revolt was limited to the south of England. This does not mean that everyone in the rest of England was happy with the way they were being treated and taxed. These were places from which a march on London looked more possible. There were outbreaks of burning and rioting in areas all over the country.

Not all the rebels came from Kent and Essex. If you look back to the map on page 78, you will see there were other places in England where the peasants were angry enough to burn barns and crops, to refuse to work for the lords of the manors on which they lived, to refuse to pay the Poll Tax and to kill those who tried to make them return to their old ways of working before the Black Death.

One of these places was the county of Suffolk. Here, if we look at the court records of the people who were brought before the justices, we can find out about the sorts of people who were desperate enough and angry enough to rebel against the old system.

WILLIAM METEFIELD OF BRANDON

William first appears in the courts in 1369, when it was said that he *drew blood* from Alice Godhewe. Eight years later he was a brewer. We know this because he was accused of brewing too much ale for sale and fined 2s. He led a band of rebels in 1381 who robbed and fought their way around south-west Norfolk. They demanded money with menaces, stole goods and attacked the Duke of Lancaster's manor at Methwold. William doesn't appear in any court records after the Revolt. What could have happened to him?

MARGARET WRIGHTE OF LAKENHEATH

We know about very few women rebels, but Margaret is one of them. Before 1381 she was a brewer. We know this because in 1379 she was fined for brewing too much ale for sale. In 1381 she joined the rebels. She was accused, with Katherine Gamen, of helping to kill Sir John Cavendish, a Royal judge. We do not know what happened to her.

JOHN HARAS OF HERRINGSWELL

We first hear about John when he was a **juror** in a general court held at Herringswell in January 1371. On 14 June 1381 he joined a group of rebels. They marched to the manor of Chippenham in Cambridgeshire and attacked it. They were arrested. John was pardoned for his crime in 1383.

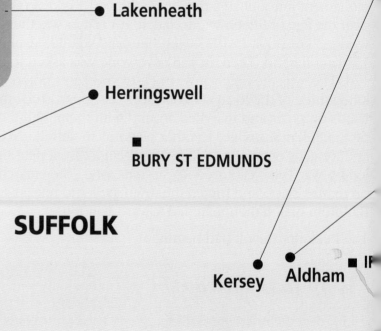

N
S

- Brandon
- Lakenheath
- Herringswell
- BURY ST EDMUNDS

SUFFOLK

- Kersey
- Aldham
- IP

0   25 mile
0   25 km

ADAM ROGGE OF ALDHAM

We first hear about Adam when he is accused of *raising a hue and cry* against his mother Matilda in 1360. This must have been a really serious family quarrel. He was in trouble again a year later for beating up Thomas Elenesfenne. In 1371 he was involved in an argument over a debt, and was fined 1s for letting cows (which belonged to four different people) stray. We can guess from this that he was a herdsman. Ten years later, he appears in the court records as a bailiff on his lord's manor. However, on 14 June 1381 Adam joined the rebels. They attacked the house of William Gerard of Watlesfield and the next day stole money from Roger Usshfeld's house.

THOMAS SAMPSON OF KERSEY

In 1364 a complaint was made against Thomas for grazing 180 sheep on common land at Polstead. By 1381 he owned land in three villages – Kersey, Harkstead and Friston – and goods worth £65.12s.8d including 161 acres of land with crops, 72 horses and cattle and one eighth share in a ship! He was not a poor man. In 1379 and again in 1381 he collected the Poll Taxes in Suffolk. However, he must have had a serious change of heart. In June 1381 he led groups of rebels in the south-east of Suffolk, stirring up rebellion in Ipswich, Melton and Bramfield. He was captured and condemned to death. At first he was refused a pardon, but was finally pardoned in 1383.

LOWESTOFT ■

Suffolk rebels

The people on these pages are just a few of the Suffolk rebels. We know about them from the court records that we have.

It would be easy to think, from reading these boxes, that the rebels were all people who were likely to get into trouble anyway.

It is important to remember that there would have been many other rebels who had led law-abiding lives before the rebellion. We cannot tell you about them, for they have left no trace.

JOHN COLE OF FELIXSTOWE

In 1363 John Cole was fined for refusing to do winter work for his lord, the Prior of Felixstowe. In 1381 John was one of a band of rebels who burned the records of the manors of Felixstowe and nearby Walton. Three years later he agreed to pay a fine of 8s for his part in the rebellion. But the court discovered that John had, some time before 1384, bought land without permission. The court was going to seize the land so John refused to pay the 8s fine. In November 1385 he was accused of assaulting another peasant. He left his manor without permission and was described by the court as a 'rebel'. He was ordered to be arrested on sight. We know nothing more about him, so maybe he got clean away.

On 12 June 1381 rebels from Kent and Essex reached the outskirts of London. The leaders of both groups met at Blackheath to discuss what they were going to do. Altogether there were about 60,000 peasants. They had few real weapons and were not trained soldiers, but they were determined.

King Richard II was only 14 years old and had no experience of dealing with problems like this. He decided to meet the rebels. On 13 June Richard and his advisers were staying in the Tower of London. Richard II, Simon Sudbury (who was Chancellor and Archbishop of Canterbury) and the Treasurer, Robert Hales, set off in the royal barge for Rotherhithe. Simon Sudbury and Robert Hales were the two men the peasants blamed for the Poll Tax. As soon as the peasants saw who was on board, they began shouting that the 'traitors' Simon Sudbury and Robert Hales should be killed. The rowers quickly turned the barge and Richard and his advisers went back to the Tower.

The rebels in London

The rebels had the support of the people of London who opened the gates of the City to them. The rebels from Kent streamed over London Bridge and those from Essex went in through Aldgate. Londoners handed out loaves of bread and offered jugs of water and ale. Then the peasants burnt down John of Gaunt's Palace and the Temple (where legal records were kept). They killed the Lord Mayor of London. Finally, they surrounded the Tower and demanded to see the King. London was in the hands of the rebels.

Source A

This medieval painting shows Richard II meeting the rebels at Rotherhithe in June 1381.

Source B

Part of a speech made by John Ball to the rebels at Blackheath on 13 June 1381. It was written down by Jean Froissart in his *Chronicle* which he finished in about 1401.

Good people, nothing can go well in England unless there is neither villein nor nobleman. The men we call lords, what makes them our masters? They wear silks and velvets while we wear poor cloth. They have wine, spices and good bread, but we eat rye and straw, and have water to drink. They live in fine manors, we sweat and toil in the fields in the wind and the rain. They call us slaves and beat us if we do not serve them. We have no one to listen to us. Let us go to the King and explain our situation. Let us tell him we want it changed, or else we will change it ourselves.

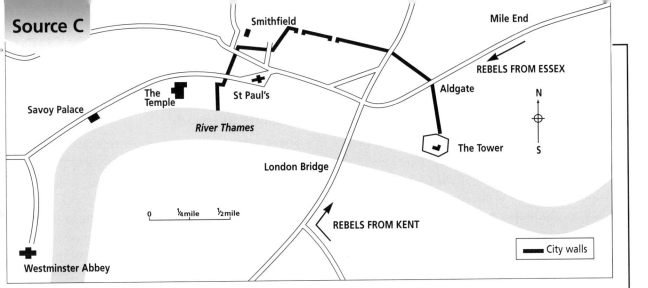

Source C

London in 1381 showing the routes the rebels took.

The King meets the rebels

The King met the rebels at Mile End, outside the City walls. Wat Tyler asked the King for four things. He said that the King should:

- abolish serfdom

- abolish all labour services

- punish his advisers

- pardon everyone who had taken part in the rebellion.

Richard agreed to everything except punishing his advisers. So the rebels decided to do that for him. They killed Simon Sudbury and Robert Hales. They stuck their heads on poles set in London Bridge. That night there were terrible riots in London.

On 15 June, King Richard II met the rebels again. This time the meeting was at Smithfield. Wat Tyler made further demands. No one quite knows what happened next. What is clear is that there was a scuffle involving Wat Tyler, the Lord Mayor of London and one of the King's attendants. Wat Tyler fell from his horse, dying. At once, thousands of peasants raised their bows, ready to fire. The King was within an arrow-shot of death. He shouted to them: *Sirs, would you shoot your king? I will be your chief and captain. Only follow me and you will have what you seek!* The peasants followed the King into Clerkenwell fields. There, he persuaded them to go home. He would, he said, keep the promises he had made at Mile End.

Broken promises

As soon as the peasants were clear of London, King Richard began breaking his promises. Wat Tyler's head was cut off and stuck on a pole on London Bridge. John Ball was caught and hanged. Thousands of peasants were fined, had their land taken from them or were hanged. The Peasant's Revolt was over.

Source D

King Richard II said this to the peasants at the end of the rebellion. It was written down by Thomas Walsingham in 1381.

Oh, you wretched men, detestable on land and sea. You who seek equality with lords are not worthy to live. Villeins you were and villeins you shall remain.

John Ball

We know very little about John Ball before he took part in the Peasants' Revolt. By 1366 (aged 20) he was living in Essex, but travelled around to preach. He was arrested many times for preaching his ideas on equality. His most famous remark is: *When Adam dug and Eve span [wool], who was then the gentleman?*

Why did the Hundred Years' War start?

Since 1066 English kings had been ruling over lands in France. By the time of Henry II, England was just a small part of the Angevin Empire. This Angevin Empire (look back at the map on page 33) was huge compared with the lands ruled by the French kings. In the 1200s, however, things changed. King John lost many lands in France and spent much of his reign desperately fighting to win them back. Would the English eventually be forced out of France? Could the English kings reclaim lands they thought were rightfully theirs?

The English invade

By 1337 the English king, Edward III, was ready to act. He invaded France and claimed the right to rule over all French lands. His mother was the sister of the French king, Charles IV, who had died without sons or brothers. Edward believed he had a better right to the throne than the man who had been crowned King of France, Philip.

Reasons to invade

There were, of course, other reasons for this invasion of France. The French were helping the Scots, who were busy sending raiding parties over their border with England. English merchants, especially those who dealt in wine and salt, were unhappy because wine and salt producing areas in France were now under French, not English control. Furthermore, Edward and his son, the Black Prince, were very keen on ideas of **chivalry**. Edward even set up a special band of knights, the Knights of the Garter. What else could a real knight do, but fight and put his ideas into practice?

A worthwhile war?

The wars that followed lasted on and off for over a hundred years. They cost a lot of money (the Poll Tax, page 79, was one of the ways of paying for them) and they cost a lot of lives. At the end, in 1455, England was left in control of only the port of Calais. All the other lands in France were lost.

Source A

A modern picture of the types of people who went off to battle and the weapons they took with them.

Cannon were used at the Battle of Crécy. Henry V had 75 gunners, who bombarded French towns.

As well as soldiers there were **armourers**, grooms, priests and surgeons. Women joined as helpers.

Some bowmen also used crossbows. These were drawn by winding a handle, and could shoot arrows through armour.

A squire looked after a knight's armour, which packhorses carried. The squire helped the knight to put his armour on.

The Battle of Crécy 1346

In 1346 Edward III sent a huge invasion fleet across the Channel to Normandy. He planned to march across northern France and capture Paris with 112,000 archers and 2,400 cavalry. However, the English met with strong resistance from a French army three times as big. The English were forced to flee towards Calais which was held by the English. But before they could get there, the French caught up with them at Crécy. On 26 August the battle began. The English had time to choose a position on high ground, rest and eat before the battle. The French army, on the other hand had had to march a long way and were tired. The French army was much bigger than the English army – some people say eight times as big. Who would win?

Jean Froissart

Froissart was born in 1344 in Hainault, in what is now France. He was a poet and historian. He is famous for his *Chronicles*. Some of the stories in this are based on personal observations, his own or those of people he talked to. But he is not always accurate. He died in about 1405.

Source B

From Jean Froissant's *Chronicles* which he finished in about 1401. He is describing the Battle of Crécy.

As soon as **King Philip saw the English**, he ordered his crossbowmen to advance. But they were exhausted after a long march in full armour. Suddenly there was a heavy shower of rain. When the rain cleared, the sun shone – but into the eyes of the French. As soon as the French crossbowmen came within range, the English archers took one step forward and shot their arrows with such speed and force that they fell like a heavy snowstorm on the French. The French crossbowmen turned and retreated in panic. King Philip saw their retreat and cried: *Kill those scoundrels for they block our path in their cowardice.* But even the French knights were now being hit by English arrows and they too fell back in confusion.

There were some Cornish and Welsh footsoldiers in the English army who were armed with large knives. They advanced through the ranks of the French and stabbed the earls, barons and knights. Their Lord was annoyed that they had killed so many, because he would now lose ransom money.

Foot soldiers wore everyday clothes. They carried their own weapons.

English archers had **longbows**, which they carried wrapped in cloth. They wore leather **jerkins** and carried food in sacks.

A knight wore steel armour, as did his horse. He carried a shield and used an axe or mace to fight hand-to-hand.

Pages served the knights. They were sometimes killed helping knights off their horses during battle.

Back to France

On 11 August 1415 the English king, Henry V, set sail for France to claim lands he thought were rightly his. He took about 6,000 skilled archers and 2,500 knights. They captured the town of Harfleur in September without too much trouble. Then disaster struck. English soldiers started dying from plague. Henry feared he would have too few fit soldiers to beat the French.

A bold challenge

Henry was young, strong and a good fighter, so he challenged the king of France's son, the Dauphin, to fight him one-to-one. The prize would be the throne of France. The Dauphin refused. He wasn't stupid! He guessed Henry was stronger and more skilled at fighting. Anyway, the French army could easily out-fight the weakened English soldiers.

The Battle of Agincourt

Henry saw that his army would have to fight. Battle lines were drawn up close to the castle of Agincourt. The English bowmen walked to within 275 metres of the French. Then they fired. The French knights were packed so close together that many were killed or wounded. The French soldiers behind had trouble getting over the mass of bodies to fight back. The English bowmen fired again and again. Then they put down their bows, took up their swords and fought hand to hand.

Source A

A medieval painting of the Battle of Agincourt.

After the battle

Hundreds of French soldiers were captured; still more were killed or fled.

Messengers then told Henry that French peasants had attacked his **baggage train.** They had stolen his crown and the Great Seal of England. He immediately had all the French prisoners of war killed. Henry wasn't troubled again either by French troops or French peasants.

Battlefield surgeons

Henry V took ten surgeons with him to France in 1415. The top surgeon was called William Bradwardine. The team of ten looked after sick and wounded English soldiers after the battle of Agincourt. What could they do in the days before anaesthetics and blood transfusions, plastic surgery and skin grafts? In fact, they could do a lot. The large number of battles in medieval times gave surgeons lots of chances to experiment and develop new techniques for treating wounds. Wounds and fractures are easy to see - and it was easy, too, to see quickly whether or not a treatment was working.

Source B is an illustration from a medical book and shows the sorts of battle wounds medieval surgeons thought they could deal with successfully. It also gives us a good idea of the sorts of weapons that were used in medieval times.

Now read Source C. This was written in the 1200s by Theodoric of Lucca. He was a skilled Italian surgeon, son of another surgeon, Hugh of Lucca, who had gone with Italian troops on the fifth Crusade, and learnt a lot about the treatment of wounds. William Bradwardine and his surgeons would almost certainly have known about, and probably used, the treatments developed by Theodoric and Hugh of Lucca.

Source B

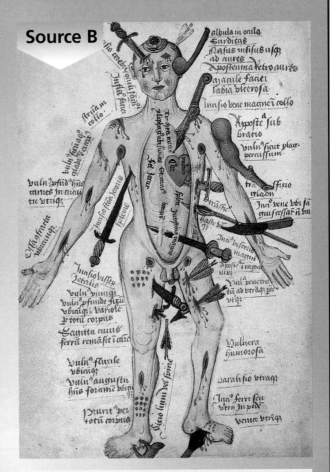

This 'wound man' is a picture from a medieval book about medicine.

Source C

Written by Theodoric of Lucca in his book *Chirurgia Magna* in the thirteenth century. His father's discovery that wine healed wounds was very important. We know now that wine is a good antiseptic because of the alcohol and acids it contains. Some surgeons carried on using ointments that didn't really work. Perhaps they hadn't heard of the new treatment; perhaps they did not believe the new ways would work.

The method used for extracting arrows cannot be described in detail for every day we see new instruments and new methods being invented by clever and ingenious surgeons...

My father used to heal almost every kind of wound with wine alone, and he produced the most beautiful healing without any ointments.

Medieval surgeons

Some medieval surgeons had read books like those of Hugh of Lucca, or had learned through contact with Arab doctors during the Crusades. Some had learned from working on battlefields. Others had not. They still cut off limbs and left patients to rot, or die of shock.

11.3 THE WARS OF THE ROSES: YORK V. LANCASTER

In 1422 Henry VI became King of England. He was a very religious man who spent many hours praying, but was not a strong character and found it difficult to control the mighty nobles in his kingdom. In 1450 a Sussex farmer said of Henry that he was: *a natural fool and no man to be ruling this land*. The farmer was put to death for his insolence, but he was soon proved right!

In 1453 Henry had the first of many attacks of insanity, and his cousin, Richard, Duke of York, was made regent. When Henry recovered he tried to continue as King, but Richard was not prepared to give up the power he had gained.

Source B

Ordinary people did not usually fight in the wars, but sometimes they were attacked by soldiers who stole from them.

Source A

Lancastrians and Yorkists all descend from **Edward III** (1327–1377)

- Lancastrians
- Yorkists
- ✕ killed in battle
- 🗡 murdered

Richard Duke of York killed in 1461

Henry VI (1422–1461) (1470–1471) married Margaret of Anjou

Margaret Beaufort married Edmund Twdwr Earl of Richmond

Edward IV (1461–1483) formerly Earl of March married Elizabeth Woodville

Elizabeth of York

Edward V (1483) died in Tower 1483

Richard died in Tower 1483

Edward Prince of Wales killed 1471

Henry VII (1485–1509) married Elizabeth of York

Henry VI was a member of the House of Lancaster, whereas Richard came from the House of York. Their dispute over who should rule England soon turned into a civil war between the two families. Later these wars were called the Wars of the Roses, because the York emblem was a white rose and the Lancaster emblem was a red rose.

Each of the families employed private armies to fight for them and for the next thirty years a series of battles was fought as first one side, and then the other seemed to have won control of the country. Ordinary people had little part to play in the dispute, and for them life continued much as it had done before.

This family tree shows you how the families of York and Lancaster were related, and what happened to them. The dates in brackets are the years they reigned.

Lancaster or York?

At first it looked as if the Lancastrians, supporters of Henry VI, would win. They won battles at Wakefield in December and at St Albans in February 1461 and Richard of York was killed. Then, in March of the same year, there was a battle at Towton in Yorkshire. It was fought in a snowstorm and raged from dawn to dusk. At the end, the river which ran through the battlefield was blocked with bodies. The surrounding meadows were flooded with blood. 28,000 men were killed or wounded on that day. The Yorkists won and Richard's son, Edward IV became king. Henry VI was forced to flee abroad.

Richard III takes over

In 1469 the Earl of Warwick, Edward IV's chief adviser, changed sides. He wanted more power and thought the Lancastrians would give him it. Warwick forced Edward to flee abroad. Henry VI became king again. Edward fought back. Yorkist soldiers killed Warwick at the Battle of Barnet in April 1471. The following month Edward won the battle of Tewkesbury and became king once more. He ruled England successfully until he died in 1483. He left his 12-year-old son, Edward V, to take over as king, but instead the King's uncle, Richard III, took over the throne. He knew that England needed a strong ruler to prevent the outbreak of more fighting. Edward was imprisoned in the Tower of London and was never seen again (see page 90).

(see page 90)

Source C

The progress of the Wars of the Roses

1422–1461
Henry VI

→ 1461–1471
Edward IV

1470–1471
Henry VI

→ 1471–1483
Edward IV

1483
Edward V

→ 1483–1485
Richard III

1485
Henry VII

→ End of the Wars of the Roses

The red boxes show Lancastrian kings, the white boxes show Yorkist kings. The dates shown are the years they reigned.

Warwick, kingmaker

Richard Neville, the Earl of Warwick, was a very powerful man in the Wars of the Roses. He was born in 1428. The whole family was involved in political plotting. They had a lot of land and large armies, so had a lot of power. Edward IV depended on the Nevilles, so gave them more and more power, to keep them happy.

Warwick's power was so great he was called 'the kingmaker' because the side he supported was more likely to win. When he deserted Edward IV for Henry VI, Henry won. Warwick was killed at the battle of Barnet in 1471.

11.4 RICHARD III - THE LAST YORKIST KING OF ENGLAND

The last Yorkist king of England, Richard III, reigned for just two years. Some say he ruled wisely and well; others that he was a cruel tyrant who murdered his two nephews and took the crown for himself.

Richard III – a wicked uncle?

Edward IV died suddenly in 1483. His two sons were Edward, aged twelve, and Richard, aged nine. Before Edward IV died, he gave his younger brother, Richard, Duke of Gloucester, the job of Protector. This meant that Richard ran the country until the young prince Edward was old enough to rule by himself. Richard of Gloucester had always been a loyal supporter of his brother Edward. He had a reputation as a good soldier and had kept law and order in the north of England where he was very popular.

Source A

This portrait of Richard III was painted in Tudor times, and is probably a copy from one painted by an artist who had seen Richard.

Then things changed. In June 1483, Richard of Gloucester announced that his brother Edward IV had never been legally married to Elizabeth Woodville. This meant their children were illegitimate, and so neither of the young princes could become king. Richard of Gloucester then took over the throne. He was crowned King Richard III in July 1483.

A Royal murder?

Rumours quickly spread that Richard had murdered the two princes. They had been living in the Tower of London, and the last time anyone saw them playing in the gardens was in August 1483. Two months later there was a rising against Richard. Richard got more and more unpopular. His supporters drifted away – many to support a young man called Henry Tudor, a Lancastrian.

In 1674 workmen found the bones of two boys in the Tower of London. Experts since have disagreed about whether or not they are the bones of the young princes.

Source B

From an account of the murder of the princes, written by Sir Thomas More in 1520. He said it was part of a confession made by Sir James Tyrrel and John Dighton when they were in prison for treason.

Sir James Tyrrel was sent to Sir Robert Brackenbury, Constable of the Tower of London, with a letter from King Richard to say that he should be given all the keys of the Tower for one night. The two princes were under the care of Will Slater, called 'Black Will' and Miles Forest, and these two, with the groom John Dighton, smothered the princes in their beds. Then rode Sir James to King Richard, who gave him great thanks.

The Battle of Bosworth Field
21 August 1485

Henry Tudor decided that his time had come. He had been taken to France – and safety – by his Uncle Jasper in 1471. He learned about warfare, treachery and betrayal, court politics – and how to gain and keep supporters. In August 1485 he landed, with around 2,000 soldiers, at Milford Haven in South Wales. He was going to claim the throne of England. Slowly he advanced through Wales to the Midlands. Steadily more and more supporters joined him. By the time he reached Bosworth Field, he had an army of about 5,000 men.

Richard had an army at least twice the size of Henry's. However, one of his commanders, Sir William Stanley, had not decided on whose side he would fight. Together with his brother, Stanley had nearly 6,000 men under his command. The side on which he fought would win. Richard, of course, did not know Stanley was thinking of changing sides.

Richard's troops took up their positions along a ridge above marshy ground. Henry's foot soldiers advanced, and battle began. Suddenly, Sir William Stanley made up his mind. He began to fight on Henry's side. Seeing this, Richard himself plunged into the thick of Henry's troops. Richard's horse galloped straight into the marsh and couldn't struggle out. Richard leapt from the saddle. He was immediately surrounded by Henry's men, who cut him down and killed him. It was all over. The battle had lasted less than an hour. There is a legend that says William Stanley found Richard's crown in a thorn bush and presented it to Henry Tudor, the new King Henry VII.

The Tudor rose is a double rose: red on the outside, white in the centre. In 1486 Henry Tudor married Elizabeth of York, Edward IV's eldest daughter. By marrying, they joined together the Yorkists and the Lancastrians. The red and white rose were one, and the Wars of the Roses were over.

Henry Tudor

Henry Tudor was born in 1457. He became king in 1485, aged 28. He had spent all his life until this point fighting or in exile. He wanted to stay king. He knew the best way to do this was to end the Wars of the Roses once and for all. He married Elizabeth of York, so joining the families of York and Lancaster. This worked.

Having settled the Wars of the Roses, Henry went on to settle the country. He had sons to take over the Tudor throne. He cut down the power of the nobles and stopped them having their own armies, so they were less of a threat. He died, not in battle, in 1509.

abbess the head nun of a nunnery or convent.

Anglo-Saxon Chronicle a record of events usually made as they happened, ordered by King Alfred of Wessex around 891 and written by monks. The Chronicle ended in 1154.

annulled the cancelling of a marriage with the consent of the Catholic Church.

apothecary the medieval man of medicine and potions similar to a modern chemist.

apprentice a boy attached over several years to the master of a trade to learn skills.

armourers skilled metal workers who made suits of armour for knights.

baggage train the column of helpers, servants, wounded and supplies that followed behind medieval armies.

bailey the outer wall of a castle protecting the outbuildings and animals.

Benedictine an order of monks founded by St. Benedict.

cellarer/ess monk or nun who kept the keys to the cellar.

chain-mail armour made of metal rings linked together.

charter a written list of rights or rules agreed between the monarch and the people.

chivalry the religious, moral and social codes of behaviour of medieval knights.

chronicles books written by monks describing daily life and events.

Cistercians members of the Cistercian order of monks that was founded as a stricter branch of the Benedictine order.

civil war a war between people of the same country.

cloisters a covered walkway in monasteries or nunneries where monks and nuns walked, worked and prayed.

craft guilds (see guilds)

crozier a hooked staff (like a shepherd's crook) carried by bishops, abbots and abbesses.

curfew a rule ordering people to stay in their houses, usually at sunset, when the curfew bell is rung.

excavations the digging of trenches in the ground to uncover ancient remains.

export a product made in one country and sold to another.

exchequer the Royal treasury, where money and funds are kept.

fealty an oath of loyalty and obedience sworn to the king.

glebe land which belonged to the church and was looked after by priests.

guilds medieval groups of craftsmen or merchants. Guilds set rules about prices, wages and practice.

hue and cry the call raised to sound the alarm or chase a criminal.

hundreds areas of land within **shires**, which each had their own courts of justice.

illuminated monks illustrated their books with detailed coloured drawings.

infidels people who were not Christians.

interdict a punishment given by the church banning people from attending church services.

jerkin a sleeveless leather jacket worn by men.

journeyman a skilled worker who is employed by a master.

keep a high tower surrounded by a wall within a castle.

legitimate a child born of parents who are married.

longbow bows, six foot high, made of yew and drawn by hand, which shoot a feathered arrow.

Mass the Catholic communion service.

master a highly skilled craftsman, able to teach others.

mayor the leader of the governing body of the town.

miracle plays medieval plays based on the Bible or the lives of the Saints.

monks men living in a community apart from the world under the rules of a religious order (see also **Benedictine** and **Cistercian**).

motte the mound of earth on which a castle is built.

nunneries buildings in which a religious community of nuns live.

poultice a warm bandage applied to draw out inflammation from wounds and boils.

ransom money demanded for the release of a prisoner.

reeves the officials in charge of the lord's estate and the villagers.

Rule of St. Benedict the code of behaviour laid down by St Benedict for Benedictine monks to follow throughout their lives.

sacristan person who looks after a church and churchyard, often acting as bell ringer and gravedigger.

shield wall a barrier of shields held up by soldiers to protect them from attack.

shires areas of land, roughly the same as modern-day counties.

shrine a chapel or altar dedicated to a saint.

tithe a tax paid to the Church consisting of one tenth of all the villagers' produce.

villeins tenants controlled by the lord of the manor.

Whitsun the Christian festival remembering the appearance of the Holy Spirit to the disciples of Jesus.

Acknowledgements

The authors and publishers would like to thank the following for permission to reproduce photographs:

Aerofilms Ltd: 1.1D
Ancient Art and Architecture: 3.1B
Bibliotheque Nationale, Paris/Bridgeman Art Library:
5.2B, 9.4D, 10.3A
Bibliotheque Royal de Belgium/Bridgeman Art Library: 8.3B
Bibliotheque Royale Albert: 9.1A
Bodleian Library: 2.4A, 3.3D, 3.5A
British Library: 1.1F, 3.4A, 3.5D, 3.6A, 5.3A, 6.1A, 6.2A,
6.4A, 8.1A, 8.2B, 9.2B 6.5A
British Library/Bridgeman Art Library: 3.6B, 4.3A, 8.2D, 10.1B
Masters and Fellows of Corpus Christi College, Cambridge: 1.1E
English Heritage: 2.2A, 3.4D
Giraudon/Bridgeman Art Library: 1.1A
Michael Holford: 2.1A, 2.2B, 2.3B
House of Commons/Bridgeman Art Library: 4.4A
A K Kersting: 3.1A
Lambeth Palace Library/Bridgeman Art Library: 11.2A
Museum of London: 3.3B
National Museum of Ireland: 7.2B
National Portrait Gallery: 11.4A
The National Trust Photographic Library: 3.4E
Scottish National Portrait Gallery: 7.4C
St Mary's Church, North Mimms: 3.2
Trinity College, Dublin: 7.2C
Wellcome Institute Library: 11.2B

The publishers have made every effort to trace copyright holders of material in this book. Any omissions will be rectified in subsequent printings if notice is given to the publisher.

The authors and publishers gratefully acknowledge the following publications from which written sources in the book are drawn. In some sources the wording or sentence structure has been simplified.

W Anderson (ed. trans.), *Chronicles*, Centaur Press, 1963: 11.1B
Christopher Brooke, *From Alfred to Henry III, 871-1272*, Sphere, 1974: 2.1B
Camden Society XXXVII, *A Relation of the Island of England, in about the year 1500*, 1847: 6.5B
John Chancellor, *Edward I*, Weidenfeld and Nicolson, 1981: 7.3A
Geoffrey Chaucer, *The Canterbury Tales*, Penguin, 1962:
3.3A, 3.5E
Ian Ferguson, *History of the Scots*, Oliver and Boyd, 1987: 7.4A
Ronald C Finucane, *Miracles and Pilgrims*, Dent, 1977: 1.1B
G N Garmonsway (trans.), *The Anglo-Saxon Chronicle*,
Dent, 1972: 4.1
R Harvey, *Medieval Crafts*, B T Batsford, 1976: 3.3C
W O Hassal, *They saw it Happen 55 BC – 1485*, Blackwell, 1965:
4.3B, 11.4B
Robert Higham and Philip Barker, *Timber Castles*,
B T Batsford, 1992: 2.5D
Rosemary Horrocks, *The Black Death*, Manchester University Press, 1994: 9.1C, 9.2A, 9.4A, 9.4B, 9.4E, 9.4F

E M C van Houts, 'The Norman Conquest through European Eyes', *English Historical Review*, 110, 1995: 2.5B
John Joliffe (trans.) *Froissart's Chronicles*, Harville Press, London 1967: 1.1C, 10.3B
E D Kirk (ed. trans.), *Piers Plowman*, WW Norton, 1990: 10.1A
Tony McAleavy, *Conflict in Ireland*, Holmes McDougal, 1987:
7.2A
William of Malmesbury's Chronicle, Bohn's Antiquarian Library, George Bell and Sons, 1853: 3.5B
Sir Hugh Middleton, *Historical Pamphlets No.4*, Order of
St John of Jerusalem, Library Committee, 1930: 3.4C
C Platt, *The English Medieval Town*, Paladin, 1976: 8.2A, 8.2C,
10.1C
Eileen Power, *Medieval Women*, Methuen, 1975: 3.6C
E Revell (ed.) *Later Letters of Peter of Blois*, OUP, 1993: 4.2B
H T Riley (ed.) *Thomae Walsingham Historia Anglicana* in part one of *Chronica Monasterii Sancti Albani*, Rolls Series, 1863-4:
10.3D
Schools Council Project, *Medicine through Time*, Book 3: 8.1B,
8.1C, 11.2C
Ordericus Vitelius' History of England and Normandy,
Bohns Antiquarian Library,
George Bell and Sons, 1854: 2.3A
E Woelfflin (ed. trans.), *Regula Monachorum*, Lipsiae, 1895: 3.4

First published in Great Britain by Heinemann Library,
Halley Court, Jordan Hill, Oxford OX2 8EJ,
a division of Reed Educational and Professional Publishing Ltd

OXFORD FLORENCE PRAGUE MADRID ATHENS
MELBOURNE AUCKLAND KUALA LUMPUR SINGAPORE
TOKYO IBADAN NAIROBI KAMPALA JOHANNESBURG
GABORONE PORTSMOUTH NH (USA) CHICAGO
MEXICO CITY SAO PAULO

British Library Cataloguing in Publication Data
Kelly, Nigel, 1954 –
    Medieval realms. – (Living through history)
    1.Middle Ages – History – Juvenile literature
    I.Title II.Rees, Rosemary, 1942– III.Shuter, Jane
    909'.07

ISBN 0 431 07194 2 hardback
ISBN 0 431 07192 6 paperback

Designed and produced by Dennis Fairey and Associates Ltd

Illustrated by Richard Berridge, Finbarr O' Connor,
John James, Angus McBride, Arthur Phillips, Piers Sanford
and Stephen Wisdom.

Printed in Spain by Edelvives

Cover design by Wooden Ark